Clare xx 06

The Googly Annual

The Googly Annual

Highlights from cricket's DANGEROUSLY funny magazine

Conceived, written and produced by:
Justin Hunt, Mark Bussell, Justin Sbresni and Mark Robson

With contributions from:
**Chris Healey, Andrew Hill, Mike Richards,
Anil Gupta, Martin Booth and Jeremy Hill**

Cartoons by:
**David Holland, Jan Darasz, Rod Green, Paul McEvoy,
Peter Walker, Peter King, Mike Goodwin,
Derek Baxter, Mick Forster and Mark Robson**

Robson Books

Many thanks to Becky for helping to sell the magazine from the start and for all her commitment and dedication to the project; Jeremy, Louise and Sara at Robson for all their hard work and support and patience.

Thanks to Matthew for all the design; Sylvia and Caroline for helping with the typing; Geoff and Bill for all their organisational help; Mike for his support.

First published in Great Britain in 1994 by Robson Books Ltd, Bolsover House, 5-6 Clipstone Street, London W1P 7EB

British Library Cataloguing in Publication Data
A catalogue record for this title is available from the British Library

ISBN 0 86051 921 X

Printed in Great Britain by Butler & Tanner, Frome and London

Designed by Matthew Evans

Things You Didn't Know About
THE MCC

1 MCC stands for Marylebone Cricket Club and not Matlock Cricket Club which frequently has parties of people arriving at the ground hoping to see a Test Match.

2 Neither should it be confused with Mick's Carpet Cavern in Luton where Mick says he is fed up with having toffee-nosed prats coming in looking to buy cricket bats.

3 There are 28,000 members of the MCC and the average age is 74.

4 During the winter of 1992 the MCC rejected a motion of no confidence in the England selectors proving once again it had its finger on the pulse of public opinion.

5 MCC were the initials of a very famous cricketer, Maurice Clive Crump, who was the first man to keep wicket in oven gloves.

6 Women are not allowed in the pavilion but a queen is.

7 The MCC's ground is called Lord's after Stefan Lord, the giant Swedish darts player.

8 Colonel John Stephenson recently retired as secretary of the MCC after 14 years. His successor is to be Major-General Montesquieu-Forskin OBE who was Conservative MP for Chardonnay Central for 9 years.

9 The club has a number of very talented people among its membership such as ex-Crackerjack funnyman Leslie Crowther, and Tim Rice who was Jesus Christ's songwriter before becoming a pop quiz panellist.

10 It is often said that if a bomb was dropped on the MCC pavilion at Lord's it would destroy the Long Room and the dressing-rooms and would probably require substantial refurbishment.

It's another great ⟨free⟩ offer from *The Googly!*

Your own special cut-out and keep...

Yes!!! You too can experience what it's like to be England's most useless bowler. Simply attach these cut-out Caddick ears to your own lugholes!

Caddick ears

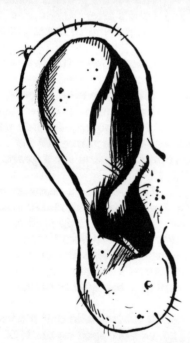 

NEXT WEEK! Your own cut-out, pull-out, pop-up Joel Garner knob!!!

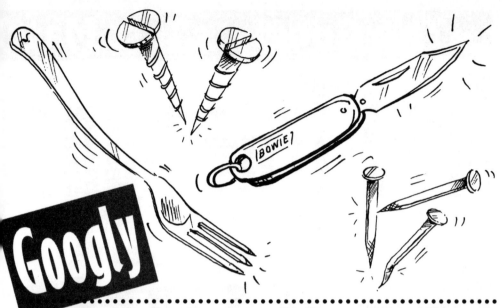

Googly

COMPETITION

Which great Pakistani bowler keeps this little lot in his kit bag?

Is it:

- **(A) Wasim Akram**
- **(B) Imran Khan**
- **(C) Waqar Younis**
- **(D) Safraz Nawaz**
- **(E) None of these**
- **(F) All of these**

Send your answers to:

**TCCB Cover-up Competition,
Alan Smith, Lords, London**

7

Fred Trueman's

RIPPING YARNS

T'were 1958, when cricketers were cricketers and not poofs in pyjamas. The Headingley sun were beltin' down and Closey's head were that red it looked like a Turk's todger after an Ottoman orgy.

I'd taken new ball and quickly run through top order with bowling that were nigh unplayable, but inexplicably I'd been taken off before I could bag all ten.

'I just don't understand what's going on out here,'

I said to Illy as our lesser bowlers toiled away. At lunch I had my customary eight pints and watched the blood seep through me socks.

I were right knackered

on account of me working the night shift down pit that week but I knew if skipper gave me pill after lunch I'd polish off those southern softies from Sussex, with their three initials, poncy white cravats, and public school ties keeping their trousers up.

All through afternoon session I were left on the sidelines as those Sussex shirtlifters edged closer and closer to our total.

I took a blinding catch round the corner of Tony Nick's trundlers, the result of hours of catching practice as a kid when I'd get our Mam to throw lumps of coal at me from two paces.

Why wouldn't skipper

Fred enjoyed a second helping

bring me on?

At tea I had another five pints and a pork pie, but then disaster struck. Young Jackie Hampshire (right poof's name if ever there was one) stood on my bowling hand with his spikes on. All me fingers were broke.

'Fred, you're on at Kirkstall Road end after tea,' skipper barked. Even though I were in right agony I said nowt about me hand. I thought I'll show ye, skipper.

Six balls later it were all over. I'd taken five wickets

> **'Yorkshire Post said it were most amazing cricket feat ever but it were nowt really'**

including a hat-trick bowling left-handed. And bloody fast too.

Yorkshire Post said it were most amazing cricket feat ever but it were nowt really. I went home and finished building our bungalow.

Trouble is, tell all this to cricketers of today and they won't believe you.

THE BALL-TAMPERER'S GUIDE TO

The top

Bottle Tops

1 Carlsberg

Probably the best bottle top in the world.

2 Boddington

Creams any Manchester batsman.

3 Heineken

Refreshes parts of your bowling attack which no other bottle top can reach.

4 Coke

If you want wickets, the coke top is the real thing!

5 Tango

Batsmen know when they have been Tango-ed.

6 Lucozade

Helps you pass quickly from the downs of taking no wickets to the ups of taking plenty.

7 Castlemaine

Ball Tamperers don't give a XXXX for anything else!

A Woman's

2 The tea pot. Check with the captain (he's probably your husband or boyfriend) what time tea is planned for and get the kettle on 10 minutes earlier. There's nothing worse than coming off the pitch and having to hang about because the tea's not brewed! Also learn the rules of the game and show a bit of initiative. If 8 or 9 wickets are down, get that kettle on.

1 Squash. Make some jugs of squash on a hot day and take them out to the players at an appropriate time. But check first that it's OK to come on. You can't just walk willy nilly onto the ground.

3 Tea towel. Get one of those tea towels with the rules of cricket on it. It provides a good conversation piece if ever another woman offers to help with the washing up.

4 Cucumber sandwiches. Traditional but still very popular. It's essential to remove the crusts.

Guide to Cricket

5 Crockery. Please. Let's have proper crockery and cutlery. None of this plastic forks and paper cups business. If you're worried about the washing up, then find another woman to help you.

6 Hot water. Have a hot jug of water to hand. Offer to rinse the players' socks if it's a hot day.

7 Cadbury's mini-rolls. An essential component of a good cricket tea. Put them out last otherwise some grubby kid will scoff them all.

8 Bread and jam. White bread – none of this brown wholemeal crap. And make it shop jam not your mother's home-made gooseberry jam from three Christmases ago.

9 Table. Choose a lightweight trestle table with foldaway legs for easy storage. We don't want it cluttering up the place when the bar opens. And if it's too heavy, you won't be able to move it.

P.MCEVOY

'The county cricket treadmill is nothing but a sex circus,' declares Gloria Rumbold, 43, the Southport landlady who has offered bed and breakfast to the game's stars since her small boarding house opened in 1973.

'I lost my virginity to a cricketer and it's been sex, sex, sex with those flannelled sex-fiends ever since.'

It all started when Northants went to play Lancashire in July 1973. Gloria picks up the story: 'A few of the Northants players stayed in my guest house and, after a long day's play, a large supper of home cooking and a few drinks, things got a bit out of hand. John Dye, the Northants seamer, may not have been much cop with the cherry in his hand, but he popped mine all right and he'll always have a special place in my heart. He was right on the spot that night and he was always allowed to bowl this maiden over whenever Northants were in town.'

Soon word got round the circuit and other cricketers were quick to jump on the bandwagon. 'Graham "Budgie"

> **'...the Northants seamer may not have been much cop with the cherry in his hand, but he popped mine all right...'**

Burgess, the Somerset all-rounder, may have been a bit slow between the wickets but he certainly wasn't slow to get me between the sheets. Graham is an umpire now and a shiver still runs down my spine when I see his finger go up.'

Players from all the counties enjoyed the special delights of a one night stay at Gloria's guest house, quaintly named 'The Pavilion'. Rodney Ontong of Glamorgan is described by Gloria as a 'tender, softly spoken man with a member like a Mozambique teddy boy' and Andy Stovold, the Gloucestershire batsman, 'liked to do it with his pads on'.

But perhaps the most notorious incident at The Pavilion took place two years ago when Hampshire were in town. 'They've always been a great bunch and a lot of fun and I wasn't expecting the full-scale orgy that they had in mind. It was really special that night

PANKY ON THE County Circuit

and the twelfth man took on an entirely different meaning for me. The champagne flowed while Paul Terry massaged my feet and Nigel Cowley got his nimble spinning fingers to work on my nipples.' But it was Raj Marv, the bespectacled slow left-armer, who turned out to be the surprise package. 'He kept going for hours and was just fantastic. I am heartbroken he's not in the team these days. But then Sussex are coming to Southport this year and Eddie Hemmings is an old favourite. He may be known to everyone else as "the whale" but to me he'll always be "honey buttocks".'

BEDSIDE CRICKET

DAVID HOLLAND

CRICKET M·A·S·T·E·R·C·L·A·S·S

TRUNDLING

by TREVOR BAILEY

Whilst it's perfectly true that the other cricketing nations have proved themselves greater exponents of the arts of pace, spin (off and leg) and even swing, there remains one area in which the English are still undisputed masters. I refer, of course, to the ancient art of 'Trundling' .

The Trundler's art is an extremely subtle area and as a result is one which often goes unappreciated, even amongst the so-called cognoscenti. As someone who has always prided himself on having been a pretty fair Trundler in his day, I can now reveal the secrets that have been passed down from Trundler to Trundler across generations.

I The run up

Not too long, not too short. Speed of approach is crucial here. The run up should be long enough to allow the Trundler to break into a lope, but not so long as to generate any real pace. Eight or nine paces is acceptable.

2 The delivery stride

A slightly longer stride than those in the run up. On no account jump into the air as this will disrupt the natural rhythm of the action.

3 The grip

The ball should be held seam up, pointing straight down the wicket. It is vital that the seam is not angled in any way and that in delivery the ball does not impart any form of spin upon it. Either of those faults could cause the ball to deviate alarmingly off the pitch. Not something any true Trundler wants to see. Also it is worth remembering that any 'shining' of one side of the 'cherry' could cause it to 'wobble' in flight, possibly even threatening movement. This is rare but can easily be ironed out by slightly altering one's action or scuffing up the shiny side.

4 Line and length

The Trundler's mantra. There is only one place for the true Trundler to put it. In terms of line it should be 'in or around' off stump and length should be 'there or thereabouts' and nothing else!

Obviously it is impossible to impart the true nature and indeed beauty of trundling in so small a space, but this shows you the basics. Perhaps now the public and indeed the selectors will appreciate this skill and soon Pringle, Cork and Topley may be as feared on the test scene as were Jackson, Cartwright, Shackleton and myself.

Sledging THE FACTS

Much has been said about 'sledging': the verbal abuse and intimidation handed out by one side against another. *The Googly* investigates...

THEN	NOW
England v Australia c1940	**England v Australia 19 August 1993**
'Congratulations, you have won the toss.'	**'Is that your face or did someone just puke up their stomach lining?'**
'Good morning umpires.'	**'Here they come; give the old cripples some room.'**
'Round of applause for the incoming batsman.'	**'If you make it to double figures, I'll eat my arse for breakfast.'**
'Umpire, would you be so kind as to hold my heavy sweater?'	**'Hold this, y'c—t.'**
'Round of applause for the outgoing batsman.'	**'I hope you can f—k better than you bat, otherwise yer boyfriend'll be well p——d off.'**
'Hard luck, England.'	**'You're all about as much use as a bag of sh—t with a hole in it.'**
'Goodnight listeners, thank you for tuning into Test Match Special.'	**'And you can f—k off as well.'**

The adventures of... A.C. Stiff
Committee Man

TO THOSE WHO DIDN'T KNOW HIM, AC STIFF WAS A MILD MANNERED MAN WHO WORKED BELOW STAIRS AT LORD'S FOR THE TCCB.

IT IS AT LORD'S THAT ALL THE BIG DECISIONS ARE MADE...

...THE ISSUE OF NEUTRAL UMPIRES...

THEN WE HAD THE ATHERTON AFFAIR. CRICKET WAS IN CRISIS BUT NONE OF THE ADMINISTRATORS KNEW WHAT TO DO.

WHAT ARE WE GOING TO DO?

...THE PAKISTAN BALL TAMPERING AFFAIR...

...THE QUESTION OF THIRD UMPIRES...

ONLY ONE THING FOR IT – WE NEED AC STIFF.

Committee Man does it again. The problems hadn't been solved. They hadn't even gone away. But they had been brushed under the carpet.

MERV HUGHES'S A-Z OF CRICKET

Arsewipe: batsman

Border: best bloody skipper in the bloody world

Chappell: other best bloody skipper in the bloody world

Donald: South African pisspot who reckons he's quick

England: poofters

Fast bowlers: real men

Gower: top Pommie. Honorary Aussie

Hick: Pommie poofter who reckons he can bat

India: darkie shirtlifters

Jones: Victorian cobber

Kiwis: New Zealand droobs who wish they were Aussies

Lara: Bastard who took 277 off us

Moustache: essential cricket gear

Newcombe: Aussie tennis player with a ripper moustache

Out: Aussie batsmen never are

Pommies: poofters

Queers: see Pommies

Richie Benaud: best bloody commentator in the bloody world

Sledging: amusing banter with the opposition

Tea: piss-up

Umpire: drongo in a white coat

Victoria: HQ of world cricket

Walk: dunno that one

XXXX: essential cricket gear

Yawn: essential requirement when England are batting

Zinc: essential cricket gear

Why THE QUEEN dislikes cricket

The Royal visit to Lord's 1993

10.30 am Arrives Grace Gates. Turned away. ('Yes, madam, and I'm Saddam bloody Hussein. No ticket, no entry.')

10.45 am Arrives Gate E. Queues with loyal subjects. Forced to buy Merv Hughes Memorial T-shirt, scorecard, *The Googly* and Cornhill Insurance hat for £17.98. At turnstile, fails to find the correct change. ('Yes, madam. And I'm the bleedin' chairman of selectors.')

10.55 am Admitted to ground at OAP rate of £27.50.

11.10 am Takes reserved seat in Mound Stand. ('Oi! You with the 'at on! Siddown dear! Siddown!')

11.15 am Large sunburnt and moustachioed colonial in string vest with 'I Love Oz' tattooed across forehead claims her seat. Forced to move. ('Hey! Missus! Siddown for chrissakes!')

11.30 am Finds pavilion. Refused entry. ('Yes, love, I'm SURE you are. And I'm the frigging president of the United States 'n' all.')

11.50 am Tries to buy beer and hot dog behind the Tavern stand. Small man in his 70s with greasy hair, halitosis and a whippet tries to chat her up. ('You always come to the match in that little yellow number then, eh? eh? Got somewhere to stay after the match, darlin'?') Same man in string vest barges past and spills beer in her handbag.

12 noon Second attempt to enter pavilion successful. Finds way to Royal Box. Chairman of MCC and chairman of selectors already installed, chanting 'Eng-er-l-and, Eng-er-l-and, Eng-er-l-and'. Asks Dexter when the first race begins. Told to sit down, shut up and award him a knighthood.

1.00 pm Presented to the teams. Gooch can't remember the names of the English players. Large, moustachioed colonial introduces himself as Merv Hughes and asks for a snog.

1.10 pm Asks where the Ladies' is. Told there isn't one.

2.00 pm Ejected from pavilion for moving behind bowler's arm. ('Yes, m'dear, and I'm his holiness the Pope.')

2.10pm Leaves for the palace.

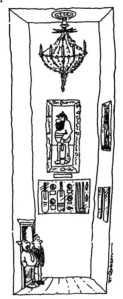

'And this is the Long Room'

Always more than happy to steal a good idea and leap on to the latest bandwagon, THE GOOGLY is proud to announce our exclusive:

Fantasy

How it works

You are a cricket selector (simply imagine yourself drunk, befuddled, spoilt, arrogant and out of touch with the fans).

It is your task to select a team. You have £10,000 to spend – a lot of money in professional cricket.

Once you have bought a squad of eleven players, had them sobered up and coached by some old, toothy fart who'd rather be running Frame Express in Taunton, you are ready to collect points based on the following rules:

● Every time a player scores 50 runs, he is awarded 4 points.

● A century is worth 10 points.

● A double-figure innings is worth 1 point but a duck loses you 2 points.

● You gain 2 points for every bowler who takes a wicket.

● 1 point goes to whoever makes a catch, even if it's a freelance photographer sitting in the crowd.

● Teams are docked 1 point for more than four bad haircuts in the side.

● Any team that fields a baldy slaphead gets an additional point.

● This increases to 2 points for on-screen swearing, nose picking or giving the umpire the finger when he isn't looking.

● Hitting an opponent (with ball, bat or fist) means a point lost, as does a dropped catch.

● Fatties falling over in the field are worth a point, especially if the ball drops on their heads after they've landed.

● Outrageous appeals and any sort of eccentric jigging, body-popping or waving of arms in a totally ridiculous fashion is worth 2 points.

● Being quoted in the newspapers as

Cricket League

..ERR.. BIJOU QUESTIONETTE BEFORE WE START... IS THIS FANTASY OR REALITY?...

EH?

Team selection

All you have to do is to choose your players from the following list. You have £10,000 to spend.

£2,000	£1,000	£500
D L Haynes	S R Tendulkar	A A Donald
R B Richardson	Javed Miandad	M G Hughes
D C Boon	I R Bishop	Wasim Akram
Salim Malik	S K Wame	B A Reid
B C Lara	M D Crowe	M E Waugh
Waqar Younis	A R Border	G.A. Gooch
C E L Ambrose	H P Tilekeratne	
A R K Kumble		

£1	10p	
M R Ramprakash	C C Lewis	
R A Smith	R J Blakey	
A J Stewart	S L Watkin	
D E Malcolm	N Hussein	
G A Hick	P C R Tufnell	
	M P Maynard	

'having it all to play for' or describing cricket as 'that sort of game' strikes 1 point from your score.

● Bolle sunglasses lose you 2 points, because they really are extremely tasteless.

● When at least 5 of your team wear stupid hats or smear sunblock across their faces, collect 2 points.

● A female streaker who bounces across the pitch while your team bats is worth 3 points. Male streakers lose

you 3 points, unless it's Chris Lewis. If Mike Gatting streaks, lose 5 points and cover your eyes.

● A player seen rearranging his wedding tackle on TV is worth 1 point.

● Derek Pringle mentioning a speed-metal band in a match review is worth a point.

● Graham Thorpe talking about how *Simply Red* help him to relax before a game loses 2.

The Googly's Book Review

It's that time of the year again and what better time than now to start scouting the bookshops for those Christmas stocking-fillers? To help save you time, here's a few that any respecting cricket lover would be proud to have in his collection.

Funnyman Willie Rushton can often be heard on radio in panel games being funny and his FUNNY BOOK OF CRICKET (Penguin £3.99) is a hilarious book about all the funny things that happen in cricket, often during Lord's Taverners games with former TV celebrities. His description of Russ Abbott playing out a maiden to Bill Wyman is very funny.

If you're looking for something a bit saucier, then recommended is Test Match Special commentator Henry Blofeld's BLOW ME! (Cape £4.50), a useful guide to oral sex - the Etonian way. Complete with illustrations and a foreword by E W Swanton, it's a must for those lonely winter evenings.

More highbrow is former *Wisden* editor Graeme Wright's latest tome in which he bemoans the commercialism of the modern game. In TREACHERY: CRICKET'S PACT WITH THE DEVIL (Faber £7.99), Wright suggests very originally that one-day cricket is bad for the game and that cricket is more commercial than it used to be.

The pick of the bunch, though, is Ken Rutherford's book on captaincy BEYOND OUR KEN (Pan £1.25). It's a very short read (only 5 pages) and in its only chapter ('Captaincy') Rutherford illuminates in no detail at all the mysteries of leading a mediocre cricket team.

'UNLEASHED'

In a SENSATIONAL new book, Graham Gooch rips the lid off cricket in a NO HOLDS BARRED EXPOSÉ. It's the publishing event of the year; 'GRAHAM GOOCH - UNLEASHED'.

On his tempestuous relationship with David Gower:

'We had one or two disagreements, but it's all water under the bridge now.'

On England beating the mighty Australians on their home turf to triumphantly take the Ashes:

'I suppose the lads played slightly better than they did on the day, but let's not forget they're a good team as well.'

On scoring his brilliant 333:

'It wasn't a bad little knock. I was quite pleased.'

On dramatically losing the England captaincy:

'Well that's cricket really, these things happen.'

On the traumatic break-up of his marriage:

'We had one or two disagreements, but it's all water under the bridge now.'

THE FIRE! THE FURY! The warts 'n' all revelations in 'GRAHAM GOOCH - UNLEASHED' published by Googly Press this Autumn.

JIMREAPER
the far boundary

MIKE GOODWIN

".... AND AS REAPER TIP-TOES IN FROM THE PAVILION END — HE APPEARS TO BE DRYING HIS HANDS ON A CHEESE-GRATER!"

THE Ghosts OF Cricke

W G Returns to Haunt Lord's

The great W G Grace – father of modern cricket – has not been seen in the flesh for centuries.

But Edna Pegg, who cleans the toilets at the MCC, claims she saw him eating a beef sandwich in the Long Room.

'It was a cold winter's night and I had finished cleaning most of the toilets. Out of season, there's not that much to do. It's different of course during the summer. I live in fear of cleaning the English dressing-room toilet when the West Indies are over.'

Bump balls in the night

Edna walked into the Long Room and spotted a fat man with an enormous beard munching a beef sandwich. 'I knew it was W G because he looked just like his photo on the wall. It's the first time I've seen a great batsman close up. He didn't stay around for long and once he had scoffed his sandwich he vanished before my eyes.'

Edna claims she has seen W G three times since then and apparently she is not alone, according to cricket ghost hunter, Professor Sherlock.

'For years I have been receiving reports of sightings of cricket ghosts. A few months ago, Fred Slate saw Len Hutton eating a hot dog outside the Headingley ground; and three years ago there was the famous Hobbs and Sutcliffe sighting. Tom Parks, 33, saw Hobbs and Sutcliffe at the pictures watching the "Rocky Horror Show", eating popcorn. The list is endless.'

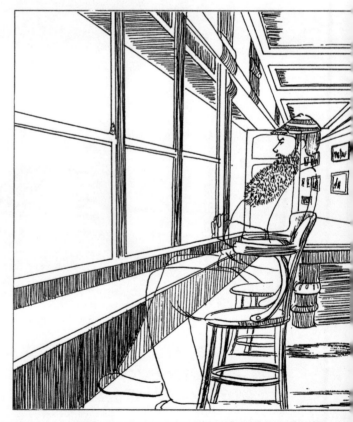

Past
Pavilion

If you have seen a cricketing ghost write to:

Professor Sherlock,
c/o The Googly
Cricket Ghost Sightings,
29b Meteor Street,
London, SWII 5NZ

and we will
PUBLISH THE EVIDENCE.

° DAVID HOLLAND °

EXCLUSIVE!! MCC orders full scale inquiry into highly-controversial claims of widespread bat-tampering in English cricket

English cricket <u>rocked</u> by

Bat Tampering Scandal

'First we had the terrible ball-tampering affair and now this enormous bat-tampering scandal. English cricket could be finished,' an MCC official said. Cricket's new enemies within, the bat-tamperers, stand accused of:

● **RUBBING** foreign substances into their bats - such as linseed oil - to improve their chances of scoring runs

● **KNOCKING** their bats in with special hammers which interfere with the surfaces of their bats so they can hit the ball further and harder

● **BANDAGING** old bats in special ways to artificially preserve their scoring performance

World class bowler, Waqar Younis, said: 'This is an outrageous scandal. Bat-tampering threatens the good name of cricket and should be stamped out at once.'

Test Match Special's Jonathan Agnew, demanded that all bat-tamperers resigned immediately - even if that meant losing some good friends. To cope with the mounting crisis, a special MCC committee is expected to make every batsman show their bats to umpires for inspection at the end of each over.

THE GOOGLY'S GUIDE TO
The Tea Lady

Age:
Prehistoric

Appearance:
Half-dead; breasts down to her knees; and a beard like W G's

Body odour:
Faint scent of lavender with traces of old English urine

Drinks offered:
Cold tea and watery orange juice

Any specialities?
A curling hair or two. Usually found in your mouth or floating on the top of your cold tea

Any extras?
Light dandruff seasoning

Favourite sandwiches:
Egg and ham

What do they taste like?
The egg tastes like cold puke and the ham like a cat's tongue

Favourite saying:
'How many for tea, luv?'

Least likely to say:
'Is "Mastermind" on tonight?'

Ambition:
To have sex with a Chippendale

If she wasn't a tea lady?
She'd be a dinner lady

Googly FREE offer!

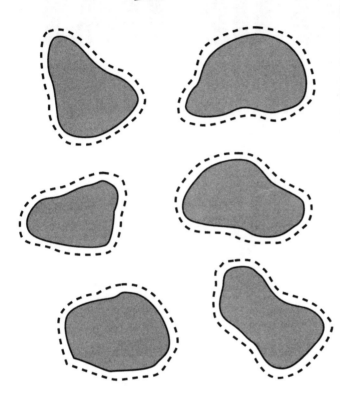

The Googly is offering you the Dickie Bird experience – the chance to feel what it's like to be the world's number one umpire. Just cut out the six pebbles – identical in shape to the ones Dickie has used throughout his umpiring career – and pop them in your pocket. Use them to count the balls in an over next time you're in the middle or just sitting at home watching cricket on TV.

HOWZAT FOR FUN?!

Third Women's Cricket International

England
◄ VS ►
Australia

**The Oval Car Park
23 September 1994**

England First Innings 62
(Minge 25, Thighs 6 for 3)

Australia First Innings 43
(k d lang 4 for 10)

England Second Innings

F S MINGE b Thighs	14
R S J CANYON-YODELLER c Navratilova b Bombdoors	1
P G DYKE c Steroids b Thighs	0
k d lang hit wicket with guitar	2
M G CELLULITE had to pick the kids up from school	
G F SLACKS lbw b Lumps	10
HUFTY hit umpire with brick	9
H P FLAPS c Thighs b Facial hair	13
P H HAM-SANDWICH came out in sympathy with Hufty	0
T HORMONES ct Flagrante Delicto b Thighs	4
D P FADGE not out	8
EXTRAS	114
TOTAL (all out)	**175**

MY KIND OF DAY

by Ray Illingworth

I get up very very early, I do. That's the Yorkshire way and it's certainly done me no harm, it hasn't. I divide my time between the Costa del Sol and Pudsey. The Costa's all right, but the food's disappointing. I bought my villa last year. It used to be part of the El Dorado set, did this villa. Got it from the BBC who used to pay my wages until I became England's cricket supremo god. I've always been a believer in two divisions for the County Championship and it's the same in my home. The first division is upstairs; the second division is downstairs. Occasionally I go to a bullfight. Watching one reminds me of the Yorkshire dressing-room when Closey was captain. I don't know much about bullfighting but after it's all over I'll go and meet the matadors and tell them how they're doing it all wrong. Then I might go on Spanish TV and tell the Spanish public how the matadors are doing it all wrong. Then I'll ring up my friends on the Spanish newspapers and tell them how the matadors are getting it all wrong. Evenings are often spent with neighbours. There are a lot of criminals on the Costa del Sol. Like the southern softie poofs who have ruined our national game for the last twenty years they are.

School match

REPORT

St Turdburglers
V
Lord Bottyspanks College

at Honeybuttocks Wood, Buggery, Devon.

The annual Cheeks Cup was once again a battle royal between St Turdburglers and Bottyspanks until a drop of the wet stuff put an end to proceedings and sent us running for cover. There we enjoyed sponge cream fingers and hot fudge macaroons and the world seemed a nice and fluffy place compared to the miserable news put out by the BBC. Who says there's a recession – there were more than enough almond slices to go round and the sherry was flowing. The early batting was a joy. Roger Fartandfallforward showed immense talent in his fluent 5 and Horace Grosvenor looked an England opener in the making with his dashing 2. The innings was marred by a selfish 92 from an overseas student who ran out poor Fforbes Montescue-Nipple and then rather hogged the show too much for my liking. He was joined by some oikish nouveau called Nash who bludgeoned a few ugly runs before we could seek the sanctuary of the cake tent.

Lord Bottyspanks	
R D O Fartandfallforward c Beaumont b de la Rue	5
H R T D L L B G Grosvenor b Carstairs	2
F C E Montescue-Nipple run out	11
The Nawab of Gwalior not out	92
C Nash not out	61
	14
	185
Extras	
For three wickets	
Rain stopped play	

Rising Cricket Stars

① The Build-up Report

One player who is bound to play for England this summer is Hick/Ramprakash/Crawley/... (other). He has shone on the county circuit and it is just a matter of time before he gets the call up and fulfils his tremendous promise.

Hick/Ramprakash/Crawley/... (other) is modest about his achievements so far.

Asked if he is ready for the pressures of Test Cricket, Hick/Ramprakash/Crawley/... (other) said, 'I am looking forward to the challenge. I am ready to play whenever my country needs me.'

When he gets that chance we can just sit back and watch one of the game's greats flourish in the arena where he truly belongs.

② The Follow-up Report (six months later)

Hick/Ramprakash/Crawley/... (other) no longer has a secure place in the England Test side. The selectors have shown immense patience but Hick/Ramprakash/Crawley/... (other) simply has not delivered.

The flaws in his technique have been exposed and quite clearly Hick/Ramprakash/Crawley/... (other) does not deserve his Test place. He was talked up by his supporters. His career is finished.

'Did they explain at the job centre that you'd be opening the bowling for England?'

Alan Lee adds...

'These do-it-yourself reports on rising cricket stars really do work and you can use them again and again, in papers such as THE TIMES. They are very useful and I don't know what I would write without them.'

A Selector

The TCCB is looking to appoint a selector. The successful applicant need not be senile but it would be an advantage. A good pacemaker is essential as is the ability to manage a hearing aid.

A proven track record in dribbling at lunchtime is desirable, any relevant experience of incontinence would be useful and the TCCB would welcome anyone who has just been released back into the community.

The successful candidate must demonstrate an understanding of the interests of the Foreign Office. If, hypothetically, a major ball-tampering matter was brought to your attention then, in that unlikely event you would be expected to do everything that Douglas Hurd told you to do in order to protect the public interest.

We also expect the successful candidate to understand the MCC's unique position in world cricket. Although the MCC no longer runs cricket, it remains the most important and useful institution in the game.

For further details contact: The House of Lords.

RAY ILLINGWORTH'S GUIDE TO

THE Bible

God:

Me

Jesus:

That Brian Lara

Lazarus:

English cricket before I took over

Heaven:

Winning a bloody test match

Creation:

When I were made Chairman

Judas:

I 'ave to keep my eye on that Boycott

Hell:

Lancashire

Plague of Locusts:

Yorkshire Cricket Committee

Joseph:

'e were inspiration for Sunday league pyjamas

Damnation:

Place where Smith and that 'ick will go if they don't get runs

Good Friday:

Depends on what t'score is

Pontius Pilate:

Ted Dexter

Harold

R ight, well I won't shilly shally about, like. I expect you're a very busy and important person – unlike me humble self – and you must have lots t'do. Steaming unbridled lust and the thrashing of sweat-soaked, gyrating bodies is, as you are no doubt aware, a normal part of everyday life in t' world of cricket. You've only got to look at the MCC to know that. But I bet you thought chirpy old Dicky never got much of a look in as far as lasses was concerned. Well, this here book is going to put you straight.

First of all, as an example, let me take you back to '74 and a lovely warm summer. So hot I had to leave me vest off for one session of a Three Day Thriller down at Canterbury. Sheila her name were. Made the tea for Kent. As soon as I saw that lass bend over the trestle to fetch me a salmon paste butty, I knew that after the final session it would be my turn to score!

MY LIFE

as the Casanova of Cricket by Harold 'Dicky' Bird, Test Umpire

Women can't resist me, you see. Can't help themselves. Apparently they sit and fantasize about me pebbles. The way I rub them and that. I tell yer, there's many an over spent rubbin' eight pebbles never mind six. But I mustn't get smutty.

So anyway, Sheila the tea lady certainly knew how to turn me urn. And I knew just how to butter her up. Have you seen *Last Tango*, like? She went after me like a dog after sausage and, three days of Kent crumpet later, I hardly had the energy to even lift me finger.

So how do I do it? How come an unprepossessing little bloke like me has to beat off the lasses with a claggy stick? What is it that makes me such a Lunch Interval Lothario and Tea Break Totty Magnet?

Well, one of my secrets is to use me eyes. It's like spotting a thin edge to first slip on a dark Tuesday in Durham. You've got to be eagle-eyed, looking for the right signs. It may be a wink, or a smile. Or then again it might be some lass rubbin' her breasts with liniment and provocatively mouthing the words 'I want you, Dicky'. That happens to me a lot. Usually on the bus home. I think standing behind the stumps all day has summat to do with it.

Yes, the lasses mentally associate those wickets with me and think my own 'middle stump' must be well worth 'batting for'. And I have to admit that, in all modesty, it is.

's Birds

But there's definitely no mini-camera in mine! Mind you, if there was you wouldn't want to see the pictures.

So, to summarise in best 'Test Match Special' form:

● Always carry a cricket stump around with you to restaurants and that and rub it a lot.

● Keep some pebbles in your pockets and play with them constantly.

● Stare at a lass you fancy until she either starts chattin' you up or calls the peelers.

Now let me tell you about my kinky threesome at Old Trafford with Miss Blackpool and Clive Lloyd. Now we all know Clive is a big man, but I have to tell you I've never seen such a massive...

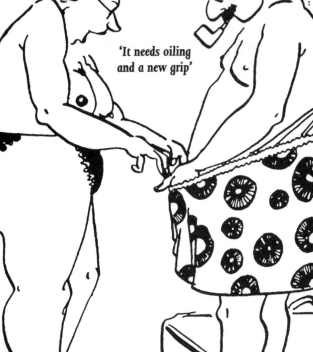

'It needs oiling and a new grip'

MY Dream Team

by Javed Miandad

(1) Chris Broad
Lovely to see a man not walking even when he's given out.

(2) Desmond Haynes
His go-slow tactics against England in 1991 were a joy to watch.

(3) Ian Chappell
Cricket owes a huge debt to this man for starting 'sledging'.

(4) Javed Miandad (captain)
True apotheosis of the perfect cricketer.

(5) Mike Gatting
I learnt a lot from this maestro's attitude to authority.

(6) Trevor Chappell
His under-arm ball will be revered for generations to come.

(7) Salim Yousuf
I still regard his 'catch' at Headingley in 1987 as the supreme example of sportsmanship.

(8) Dennis Lillee
No hard feelings against the man who gave me a kicking.

(9) Colin Croft
What can one say about a man who barges into an umpire?

(10) Aquib Javed
That sweater routine made me weep with pride.

(11) Philip Tufnell
Caught my eye when swearing at his wicketkeeper for dropping a catch. One to watch.

Change and controversy at the top of cricket

TCCB to get rid of its famous carpet

English cricket's top ruling body, the TCCB, has announced a 'radical break from the past' – they are going to get rid of their famous carpet.

A TCCB spokesman told *The Googly* that the famous carpet's days were over. 'For years and years,' he admitted, 'we have been sweeping highly controversial cricket reports under the carpet.

'But today, after the ball-tampering scandal and all the fans' worries about what is going on at the top of cricket, we have decided to buy a BRAND NEW CAR-PET – much bigger and stronger than the old one.

'We are confident that we will be able to brush everything under this one – even Beefy Botham if his forthcoming memoirs make outrageous allegations of gin-ridden, out-of-date officials running the game.'

The BIG NEW TCCB carpet measures an astonishing 1,500 metres by 1,500 metres and was specially commissioned by Alan Smith Enterprises.

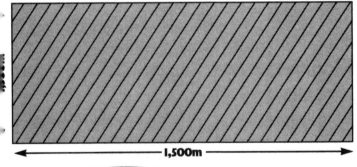

◄ **The big new TCCB carpet (artist's impression, not to scale)**

◄———— 1,500m ————►

▲ **The TCCB's Strong Lid for Very Serious Cricket Controversies (Another artist's impression)**

'If the carpet fails we have already put in an order for a special back up – a very strong lid,' declared the TCCB spokesman. 'In an emergency – if we can't sweep a controversial cricket matter under our big new carpet at least we should be able to keep the lid on it.'

My KIND OF DAY

By Mike Gatting

Obviously I get out of bed in the mornings.

Obviously I prefer home games, because obviously I don't like hotels any more – the standard of room service has gone down. I don't bother with breakfast much, just a quick piece of toast with a slice of bacon, sausages, tomatoes, fried bread, scrambled eggs, black pudding, rump steak, roast chicken and a rack of lamb. Then it's off to the bank and the Foreign Exchange till, where I change some krugerrands into sterling.

At the ground, I have to check all the players are there. Embers is usually writing love letters to Goochie, Tuffers can always be found practising his roll-ups, Desi Haynes and I often have a chat. Desi's a joker – he always says if we were in South Africa he wouldn't be allowed to play in the same team as me. I laugh and give him extra fielding practice.

Finding out what's on the menu for lunch and tea is also the captain's responsibility, and one I take very seriously indeed.

They tried to cut back the lunches at Lord's to four courses but they backed down when I threatened to resign.

Obviously I always find out who's umpiring that day as well. Most umpires are tremendous, but occasionally they're cheating bastards from Pakistan who wouldn't know an lbw if it sat up and gave them a haircut.

After play, I usually have a pint or seven with the lads, and then go home to the family. Supper's a light affair – just salad, roast beef, Yorkshire pudding, potatoes, parsnips, carrots, rump steak, roast chicken and a rack of lamb.

And then to bed with a book. At the moment I'm reading Madhur Jaffrey's Indian Cuisine (no prawns).

Mystery Bowler
COMPETITION

Can you identify the England slow left arm bowler who has just had an appeal turned down?

Answers to:
Tufnell Competition,
The Googly,
29b Meteor Street,
London SWII 5NZ

DAVID HOLLAND

WHATEVER HAPPENED TO...

Mark Ramprakash

Mark Ramprakash was a Middlesex batsman with a fiery temperament who played for England, touring in the West Indies in 1994. He then disappeared from the England scene completely, though he continued to play for Middlesex with some success.

Nowadays he still plays the odd game for Middlesex but is studying to become a barrister, where he feels he can employ his argumentative skills more usefully. 'I'm not bitter,' he says, 'but it pisses me off that that twat Illingworth didn't give me a chance.'

ARE YOU ONE OF Cricket's

1. You are bowling flat out but you cannot get rid of the opposition's last batsman. Suddenly you bowl a slower one and the ball hits his pad. It's a plum LBW. You appeal ecstatically, believing the game is over, but the umpire does not give that batsman out. **Do you:**

a Kick the stumps down and tell the umpire to piss off and get his eyes tested.

b Take your sweater, mutter to youself and go to your fielding position, shaking your head in utter disbelief.

c Bite your lip and show no emotion. You know the umpire's decision is always final.

2. You are batting and your partner calls for a quick single but you see a fielder racing in. Before you know it, you are run out. **Do you:**

a Tell you partner to f– off.

b Sigh and remind yourself that cricket is a funny old game.

c Walk vigorously back to the pavilion, putting on a brave face, determined not to be affected by such a rotten piece of luck.

Cricket is a game which sets very high standards — higher than any other sport. Unlike football, cricket is a game played by gentlemen who often eat cucumber sandwiches and wear white floppy hats. Do you have what it takes to be one of cricket's gentlemen? Just answer these questions and then check your score.

3. You are doing a spot of umpiring and the batsmen are becoming irritated because the right score is not being put promptly on the scoreboard. You politely ask the scorers to put the right score up. Two overs later, the score is still wrong. You ask again. Three overs later the score is still wrong. **Do you:**

a Run screaming from the pitch, kick down the scorebox door and strangle the scorer until he begs for mercy and promises never to be late with the score again.

b Tell the batsman to calm down and have a quiet word with the opposition's captain.

Gentlemen?

c Wander over to the scoreboard and say 'Excuse me, chaps, but can we get the score up just a jot earlier?'

4. It's the tea interval and you are starving. You are stuffing your face with an egg sandwich when you suddenly realise that the eggs are bad.
You feel sick.
Do you:

a Spit it out and slap the tea lady across the face.

b Discreetly remove the sandwich and its contents from your mouth with the help of a napkin.

c Swallow the sandwich in one to avoid hurting the dear old tea lady's feelings.

5. You are watching a Test Match. It is a hot sunny day and nothing is happening in the game. You are starting to feel restless. A supermodel in shorts walks by and the crowd begin to wolfwhistle and shout at her.
Do you:

a Tell her to get her tits out.

b Pretend not to notice what is going on.

c Draft a letter to the The Cricketer complaining about the depravity of the modern-day cricket spectator, take photographs of the base yobs and report them to the stewards.

6. You are at first slip and second slip drops a sitter. It's the fourth he has dropped that day.
Do you:

a Tell him he is probably the biggest spastic you have ever met.

b Say: 'Hard luck, Jim, good try.'

c Say: 'It's just not your day, is it, Jim. I'm sure you'll get the next one.'

January

What a bastard of a month. Stuck in a crappy hut in some foul sweater your mother's bought from Poundstretcher. Freezing your albert's off waiting for the snow to stop long enough for you to nip out and shove a dead rat up the pavilion heating duct.

You haven't even got any poxy cricketers to shout at. Oh no, they're all fannying about at some beach barbecue doing the lambada with local beauty queens all greased up and ready to go.

At least, if they're not shagging up the turf, that's all I can be thankful for.

February

Cuffing dreary. Why does the shagging weather get worse in February? We've had Christmas, haven't we? By February we should be putting out the bloody deckchairs. But no. You're back in the hut re-reading the Cricketers' Wives edition of *Fiesta* for the thirtieth time and having J Arthur competitions against the old geezers from security.

March

Early signs of weeds?! Not half. Two more months and those pansy-arsed cricket-playing gits will be back making your life a cuffing misery.

You might like to spend a bit of time sharpening up your garden fork and dreaming of turning that oily-haired Oxbridge captain into a doner kebab.

April

In April I like to break into the MCC board room and nail a dead fish to the underside of the table.

May

A deep-seated well of hatred stirs and percolates up through my soul. It erupts primevaly in tortured, half-formed words:

'Oy! You white polyester-slacked shagbaskets! Get off my cuffing pitch!'

ricketing calendar

There's only one way to treat cricketers and it probably involves them falling down with a four-wheel drive power mower, cackling wildly into the hot spring air.

June

My mind tends to go a bit black. Some of the junior ground-keeping staff whose brains haven't quite developed fully do suffer badly. They can't come to terms with why these grammar school gits are allowed to run all over the turf my lads have spent months tending, caressing and fondling. It's like watching someone in spiked boots dance on your pet hamster. A few of the lads take to making voodoo dolls and throwing hexes on the players to injure them or affect their form. Generally it seems to do the trick.

July

A good month for those stress relieving activities that keep ground staff happy. Like breaking into the changing rooms and applying fistfuls of Ralgex to the insides of boxes and thigh pads.

But don't bother peeing in the players' bath; they'll do that themselves.

August

That month where you spend half the time pulling the cuffing covers onto the pitch and half the time pulling the bastards off again. And do the players help?

Do they bollocks.

No, they all twot off for a nice cup of tea out of the nice china that we aren't allowed. Slapping each other on the back and telling each other how talented they are while above their heads is probably a picture of some geezer from the fifties who actually knew how to bat and bowl without turning into a sack of shit after ten overs. The perfect month for slashing the tyres on their sponsored Lexuses.

September

Relief in sight. Last month of the season. Most of them'll soon be poncing off back to their part-time PR jobs or whatever non-existent post some crawler who runs an estate agency has offered them.

The lucky few get the chance to spend the winter abroad, losing a few Tests on our behalf.

October

Cuffing magic. No cricket. A chance at last for the groundsmen to be truly alone with their turf. A time for healing and regrowth, for taking delivery of an exciting range of seed catalogues, for filling your underpants with John Innes No. 3 and being at one with nature.

November

Groundsman of the Year Awards. Usually held in a strip club in Rotherham. Awards like Most Interesting Ingredient in Compost (ex-cricketers are a popular choice), Most Disgusting Overalls or Smelliest Hut.

A chance for groundsmen everywhere to swap stories and interesting smells. November is, I'm afraid, the time to take that annual bath.

December

Christmas. Another cacky pullover.

Fine wines

Australian Wines

The new masters in wine production. A bit vulgar for some palates, but there's no stopping the relentless drive of these young pretenders made good.

Merv Criquet 1993
(non-vintage)

David: A bit of a bruiser, but pretty tasty none the less.

Alan: Yis mate. Stand well back when this little bugger pops his cork.

David: Would you say it's not in the same class as a Maison Lillee 77?

Alan: Not to his face.

Old Mother Boon's Date and Prune Wine
(drink before date on the bottom)

David: Marvellous.

Alan: Guaranteed to give you the runs.

Taylor's Port 1993

David: Another vintage year. You can't beat this.

Alan: We can't beat any of the buggers.

David: Language, Alan. As with the Border Bordeaux, this seems to get better every year.

Pakistan Wines

Being an Islamic state, good wines are a little thin on the ground, rather like grass on their pitches, or decent umpires.

Maison Akram 1992

David: Ah, an invigorating and powerful concoction from the dry, flat lands of Karachi.

Alan: Let's try a drop ... wait a minute, it looks like the cork's been tampered with.

David: Really? (sniffs) Oh dear, smells like it's on the turn.

Alan: Here, mate, what's Akram backwards?

David: I don't know, what is 'Akram' backwards?

Alan: Still faster than Chris Lewis.

New Zealand Wines

Since the master vintner left the company, these wines simply haven't reached anywhere near their previous high standards. Which is probably good news for the English manufacturers.

Chateau Bungy 1990

David: A decent drop.

Alan: If a bit rubbery.

Cotes de Anchor 1987

David: A very buttery taste.

Alan: You're joking mate. It tastes like cow's piss.

English Wines

Due to problems in the grape selection, the entire year's stock has turned to vinegar. It is hoped that one or two bottles may be saved in time for the winter exhibition, but we doubt it. It seems certain that the major prizes will go to the quality rum producers of the West Indies.

& Beers

Beers

Small's Stout

David: A reliable little number, still giving its best.

Alan: I don't like the shape of this bottle, though.

David: Why ever not, Alan?

Alan: It's got no neck.

Warne's White Nose Lager

David: Talking of bottles, this one's a little garish, but there's no mistaking that rich aroma ...

Alan: Wasn't me, mate.

David: ... of a classic brew. Not to everyone's taste ...

Alan: It's certainly not on Robin Smith's Christmas list.

David: ... but the sort of strong drink that'll leave you leg-stumpless.

'What d'yer mean? This IS his shortened run!'

Cheers. Nice one. Now, being a top-flight cricketer is a very demanding and physically exerting job, innit. 'Cause you've got to run about and throw balls and wotnot.

But if you're a bit of a diamond geezer spin bowler like me, you can say 'rollocks' to all that malarkey. I mean, think about it; what do spinners actually do?

1. Fielding

We fanny about on the boundary sneaking the odd oily when no one's looking. Easy.

2. Batting

We go in at number eleven, avoid the bowling, and get out sharpish. Lovely.

3. Bowling

We jog up to the crease, lob the ball, watch it fly over the boundary, and repeat until sent back to fielding. Sweet as a nut.

Thirty overs of that then it's *The Lagers*, *The Dogs*, *The Curry* and *The Late Night Jiggy-Jiggy Movie On German Satellite*. Cushty.

The Phil Tufnell Workout

◄This one's called 'The Umpire Giving Me the Ump'. Stand with yer hands on yer hips, imagine the umpire's just turned down another leg before - even though it was dead 'pudding and', then shout in a loud voice 'You what? You what? You what, you what, you what?'. Do that about a dozen times, like what I manage in the average over.

▶This is a good one for the back and legs. Pretend you're walking and pushing an object in front of you. This is one I have to do from time to time called 'The Drinks Trolley'.

RG

Meanwhile, yer fast bowlers are flat out on a physio's 'Clark Gable' somewhere, completely cream-crackered, getting X-rayed, ice-packed and Ralgexed up. What a mug's game that is.

But I suppose you've got to make a few sacrifices, know what I mean? Silk Cut instead of Marlboro, 4X instead of Stella, dansak instead of vindaloo ... and, I'm sick as a hound to have to tell yer ... you've got to put a brave face on and do a bit of exercise.

But there's exercise and *exercise*. I mean, there's only so many squat thrusts you can do before your brain turns to shredded wheat. Look at Hicky, for gawd's sake.

So, to keep the captain off yer back, I've come up with **Tufarobics** for those of us with better things to do than ponce about in lycra or push lumps of metal up and down in some manky gym.

So fags out, put *The Sporting Life* down and have a bit of a get fit jolly up with 'The Cat'.

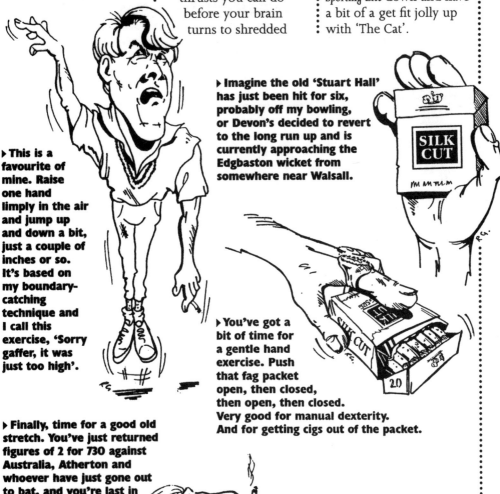

▶ **This is a favourite of mine. Raise one hand limply in the air and jump up and down a bit, just a couple of inches or so. It's based on my boundary-catching technique and I call this exercise, 'Sorry gaffer, it was just too high'.**

▶ **Imagine the old 'Stuart Hall' has just been hit for six, probably off my bowling, or Devon's decided to revert to the long run up and is currently approaching the Edgbaston wicket from somewhere near Walsall.**

SILK CUT

▶ **You've got a bit of time for a gentle hand exercise. Push that fag packet open, then closed, then open, then closed. Very good for manual dexterity. And for getting cigs out of the packet.**

▶ **Finally, time for a good old stretch. You've just returned figures of 2 for 730 against Australia, Atherton and whoever have just gone out to bat, and you're last in so it's time for a quick 'cat' nap. Not too long, though. England innings do tend to be shorter than most, don't they?**

EMERGENCY

When England are THRASHED, it is very difficult for top cricket hacks to write a match report which does not make English cricket fans feel suicidal. Here are some vital tips for cricket journalists on what they should write if England, as usual, are completely slaughtered

1 Blame the toss of the coin.

2 If England bat second, emphasize how the ground has 'mysteriously deteriorated'.

3 Question the standard of the pitch and ask if it is a suitable playing surface for first-class Test matches.

4 Emphasize the opposition's slow over rate.

5 If England's batsmen collapse, as per usual, really hype up the performance of any individual who gets over 20.

6 If no England batsman gets more than 20, try to build a story around a plucky tailender being persecuted by the opposition's fast bowlers. This will help to distract readers' attention from the awful result.

7 Try to give the impression that mysterious forces out of England's control were at work in this match. Use expressions like: 'the omens were grim' or suggest the defeat was 'fated' to happen.

8 Spend a lot of time on controversial umpiring decisions involving key English batsmen.

9 If one of England's best batsmen was clean

PMS

TIPS FOR CRICKET HACKS

12 Put the horrendous result into context by using phrases like, 'Many a one day innings has collapsed after ...'

13 Draw attention to the deliveries which 'should have dismissed' the opposition's batsmen.

14 Finish off by stressing how much England are suffering and how badly they need a win to boost their morale. Even when you know there is and never was anything there to boost.

bowled playing a totally crap shot, say he 'played the wrong line'. It sounds better.

10 If a key English bowler bowls a series of full tosses and is utterly massacred by the opposition's batsmen, write that his 'length was variable'.

11 Suggest that the opposition's batsmen, who scored 1,000 runs, were allowed to settle in and then were, of course, 'impossible to contain'.

PMS

Lewis &

Hair Care

'They're a damn sight better than ow

EYEBROW EXTENSIONS

**As worn by Trueman and Lewis.
Reet good follicular fun**

*Don't be a
southern
jessie, get
yerself some
manly northern
eyebrows*

BEFORE

AFTER

£12
PAIR

THE TONY TOUPEE

*A stylish hairpiece made
from 100%
polycarbonate resin.
Unbreakable.
Wear instead of a helmet*

PRICE
25
GUINEAS

Trueman
Products

hat's about these days, I can tell yer'

MOUSTACHE COMBS

FRED'S HAIR OIL

PRICE **£2** OLD MONEY

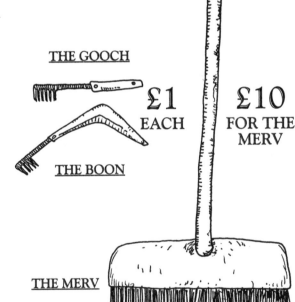

THE GOOCH

£1 EACH

£10 FOR THE MERV

THE BOON

THE MERV

Keep your facial fungus tidy and trim

Rub it on yer 'air before the match, then rub it from 'air to ball during. Result: swinging ball and swinging hairstyle

David Ward (Surrey) was in the first ever commercial shown on ITV in 1955.

Ole Mortenson (Derbyshire) is Danish for Hans Christian Andersen and is also an anagram if you are dyslexic.

In 1956 David Niven (Scunthorpe Grammar School Old Boys 2nd XI) was originally selected to play in the Old Trafford test but was replaced by Jim Laker (also Surrey) after Mr Niven strained his moustache whilst filming 'Carry On Up The Guns of Navarone'.

The Nawab of Pataudi (Sussex) played the hospital orderly in the James Bolam TV comedy classic (and misnomer) 'Only When I Laugh'.

Alan Igglesden (Kent) was also in 'Only When I Laugh'. He was an extra lying in bed opposite the aforementioned James Bolam. Iggy was the only one not acting.

Ranji (Can't remember as I'm not old enough) and not (as is commonly believed) Brian Robson is the star sporting celebrity who will stand in on 'Question of Sport' should any of the planned guests fail to attend.

John Reginald Halliday Christie (Rillington Place Old Girls CC) once knew a bloke who looked like Ravi Shastri (Glamorgan).

JIM REAPER the far boundary

MIKE GOODWIN

LORDS CRICKET GROUND

REMEMBER TO DRY YOUR HANDS!

DIRT

Hair today...

A photograph of W G Grace hangs on the wall of Ricky Costello's hair salon next to the Oval tube. It is perhaps cricket's hairiest sight, apart from a Curtley Ambrose bouncer, and is Ricky's motivation in tending to the pates of the world's cricketers.

'I've been open here since 1983 and my first cricket client was Ian Botham,' says Italian-born Ricky. 'He came into my salon wanting some highlights to give a bit of life to his footballer's cut and ever since then Beefy has been a regular and introduced many of his friends.'

Ricky's most difficult customer has been Durham opener Wayne Larkins. 'When he first came I realised he was going bald very fast but we've managed to arrest the hair loss by grafting his own pubic hair back onto his scalp. That's why it looks so frizzy.' Wayne adds: 'I feel a bit of a nana in the showers but at least I've got something to keep the sun off my head.'

Apparently Shirley Temple look-alike David Gower has recently enquired about the treatment.

It's Ricky who is responsible for Robin Smith's 'judge' look and Alec Stewart's bouffant, while Mike Gatting comes in once a month to have his 'beaver' beard trimmed. 'Mike is very fussy about his beard. He uses pictures from some of the magazines we keep lying around the salon to show how he likes it.'

But all is not sweetness and highlights in Ricky's salon. 'We had a nasty incident with Viv Richards recently. Viv came in and I was too busy with another client. I was re-gluing the dyed ferret Merv Hughes keeps under his nose. So I suggested my Pakistani assistant Aftab look after Viv. Well, Viv's not got much on top any more and basically he just comes in to have it shined but imagine my surprise when Aftab starts spitting on Viv's head and roughing it up with a bottle-top!'

But on the whole business is booming for Ricky, especially in the shaving department. 'Things have gone well for me recently. Ted Dexter has bought shares in the salon and now that Illy is in charge, stubble is a thing of the past.'

> Ricky Costello is the hairdresser to the cricketing stars of the world. *The Googly* talked to him about his heady lifestyle at his salon.

...gone tomorrow

MY Greatest Innings

by Mark Ramprakash

Obviously in a Test batsman's career there are going to be a number of innings that bring a warm glow on their recall. I've made several double figure scores in my time, but probably the innings that gives me most pleasure is the 8 I made against the West Indies in 1992.

Coming in at the fall of an early wicket, on a pitch offering occasional lateral movement, I knew I had to dig in. Having said that, I believe a bad ball should get the same treatment at any stage of your innings – so I hit my first ball, a full toss, firmly through the vacant extra cover area.

1 not out, and the perfect start. With an innings as long as this, obviously you don't remember too many details; but a collage of images remains. Surviving several loud LBW shouts; keeping out some very rapid half volleys;

regaining my mental toughness after being dropped a couple of times at slip (the bowler even called me a plucky bastard); playing out an entire maiden at one point; and my favourite memory, a cheeky cover drive through fine leg for four.

Of course, it had to end sometime, and when my epic 25-minute vigil finally did come to a close amid cartwheeling stumps, the bowler was kind enough to say that he'd thought it was never going to happen. As I left the field to typically understated applause (I love that English reserve), I little knew how much I had achieved; in the dressing-room, some team-mates even suggested that I might as well quit Test cricket there and then.

I knew it was a great innings, but I hadn't realized it was THAT good.

India

A tightly fought Ranji Trophy was finally won by Tamil Nadu in an absolute thriller at the Sharwoods Spice Factory Recreation Ground, Rajkot.

Batting first, Tamil Nadu scored 3,807 - 4 wkts dec. On a pitch that gave a lot of help to the bowlers, Tamil Nadu were rocked on to the back foot by a terrifying burst with the new ball from Panda Kar, who took 2 for 906 as Tamil Nadu collapsed to 1,756 - 2 wkts.

But seven-year-old debutant, Mornin Chundah steered Tamil Nadu to maximum batting points with an unbeaten 1,100.

In response Bombay scored 2,512 all out, narrowly avoiding the follow on but Tamil Nadu were to win when on the 43rd day of the match, six of Bombay's players had to sit their common entrance exams. The one disappointment in an otherwise enthralling domestic season was the increasing popularity among spectators of one-day games.

FUTURE ENGLAND TOURS

The TCCB have just released the tour schedules for England. The last visitors currently pencilled in to tour here are Australia and Australia is the last place to be toured in 2002/3. No further tours have been organised. However, there is a great danger that after 2001 a promotion and relegation system will be adopted and a leaked document has arrived at the chief editorial offices of The Googly that shows where England will go after 2002/3 and who will visit us here in the unlikely event of us doing a Sheffield United. So make sure that passport's up to date and your flackjacket's properly ironed.

Visitors to England

2003	Sudetenland
2004	South East Tibet
2005	Vatican City (A team)
2006	Govan
2007	A Marauding Mongol Horde XI

MCC Tours

2003/4	Bournemouth
2004/5	Ho Chi Mihn City
2005/6	Chernobyl (West)
2006/7	Black Forest Gateau
2007/8	Neptune
2008/9	Windsor Castle

'Me? I don't need pension plan,

That's what I used to think. But now look at me: 36 and on the

Mr D G is one of the lucky ones. He knew it was never too early to start making plans for the end of his career. That's why he signed up with Lord's and our tailor-made pension scheme:

The MCC Athletic Support and Abdominal Protection Fund

Specially designed to provide for you and your family when those glory days at the crease are no more than a memory (albeit a pretty recent one).

All right, you're probably thinking, I may be in my late 30s and I am going bald. But the hair that's left is still blond and curly. Well, sort of. And anyway, come off it – I

have scored over 8,000 runs in test matches.

But these days, that's just not enough.

That's where the MCC comes in. Let us answer your questions:

What do I have to do?

The principle is simple. All we ask is that starting at an early age – say 15 or 16 – you invest regular amounts of time and talent in our fund.

What then?

As you grow older, we at Lord's decide when you should increase your investment – summer or winter we'll be there to tell you that you have to spend most of your time with us. In due course, you will probably want to make a few lump sum commitments: you might, for example, decide to plough

your health, social and family life into the fund.

That's what Mr G G of Essex did . He says he has 'no regrets' about successive winters spent away from wife and children. Thanks to the MCC, Mr G G is now a 40-year-old divorcee who runs a loss-making pub, The Weary Jock Strap, in Chelmsford.

You what?

Yes, that's right! It sounds too good to be true, but the MCC undertakes not only to take away the best years of your life, but also to junk you when you still think you've got a few seasons of useful play left in you.

So what about all those years I've invested?

Well, one day, after paying you a pittance to represent your county for nigh on

to start a
'm too young ...'

15 years, some old buffer from our board will call you up and say something like: 'Sorry, David old chap. Can't offer you a place. Got to make room for the youngster, y' know.'

And then?

And then, well, you're basically free to do what you like. You could try some commentating, but, let's face it, it's pretty galling when you think you could still be out there notching up a double-hundred against the Windies. Alternatively, you could start up a small sports shop and go bankrupt within 18 months, or you could get some bored hack to ghost a biography that nobody will read.

There are no benefits at all, then?

Not really. People do still stop you in the street sometimes to ask for your autograph – if they can remember who you are.

So what do you suggest I should do to safeguard my future?

Steer clear of test cricket for starters. I hear accountancy

is a pretty reliable bet.

If you wish to join thousands of members of the MCC's retirement provision scheme, you must be a bloody fool.

Simply cut out this advertisement then, using glue and warm water, shape it into an effigy of one of the England selectors. Allow it to dry and then burn it.

'Good to see Gower back in the nets'

Pakistan

by Owt Dur Khazi

With the test team busy on duty in Australia, Zimbabwe and New Zealand plus tournaments in Sri Lanka and Sharjah, the domestic season offered opportunities to some of the up-and-coming players in Pakistan and a number of magnificent performances were noted.

United Bank's opener, Ped-ul Bin, topped the batting averages scoring 3 centuries. He shared in three partnerships of over 200 with his captain and fellow opener Fuzzifelt Circuz, both of whom went on to represent East Zone.

The sixteen-year-old Funsize Marzbarz also scored heavily making over 500 runs for Railways and with Manhole Kuvah, who made his debut for Karachi Blues at the age of nine scoring a double hundred against PIA, these two represent the future of Pakistani cricket.

Wicketkeeper Bolin Ali took 16 catches, a tournament record while Kno Khan Do held over 10 catches at slip for Habib Bank. Pick of the bowlers were slow left-armer, Jamtartz (13 wickets at 17.86) and Mustafa Kunt (12 wickets at 12.89). But without doubt the player of the season with over 600 runs and 16 wickets was PIA's Liq Hisnob.

QUAID - E AZAAM TROPHY WINNERS

Year	Winner	Year	Winner
1958	Railways XI	1976	Habib Bank
1959	Habib Bank	1977	Abbey National
1960	Habib Bank	1978	Londis
1961	Habib Bank	1979	PIA
1962	United Bank	1980	Spudulike
1963	Railways XI	1981	Spudulike
1964	United Bank	1982	United Bank
1965	United Bank	1983	Pizzaland
1966	PIA	1984	Dolcis
1967	PIA	1985	Habib Bank
1968	Railways XI	1986	Tie Rack
1969	Karachi Blues	1987	PIA
1970	Habib Bank	1988	PIA
1971	United Bank	1989	Saxone
1972	PIA	1990	United Bank
1973	Spudulike	1991	John Menzies
1974	United Bank	1992	Railways XI
1975	Karachi Blues	1993	Spudulike

THE GOOGLY'S GUIDE TO
Nicknames

The joshing that goes on in cricket dressing rooms is legend. Here are some of the more catchy nicknames

Paul 'Nosey' Parker
Chris 'Jerry' Lewis
Phil 'Beryl' Bainbridge
Robert 'Jack' Russell
Robin 'Judge' Smith
Mike 'FEC' Atherton
Paul 'Not' Allott
Graeme 'Foxy' Fowler
Angus 'House of' Fraser
Alec 'Beef' Stewart
Steve 'Kropotkin' Watkin
Phil 'Park' Tufnell
Ian 'Cathedral' Salisbury
Nasser 'Saddam' Hussein
John 'Creepy' Crawley
Mark 'Win' Illot
Nigel 'Richard' Briers
Mike 'Fat Git' Gatting
Mark 'Second World' Waugh
Allan 'North of the' Border
Mark 'Bespoke' Taylor
Jimmy 'Family' Adams
Dean 'Keeping up with the' Jones
Carl 'Turner Overdrive' Rackemann
Ian 'of Durham' Bishop

QUIZ PAGE

Across

1. Still England's best chance of winning the Ashes (6)
4. Polished Hampshire seamer (5)
7. Schoolboy abbreviation of leg before wicket (2)
9. Describe game played under floodlights in Oz (3-5)
11. Russian calling for a nun? (2)
12. Disastrous tourist to India (see 2 down for namesake) (6)
13. Ladies will have difficulty in finding one of these at Lord's (3)
14. Ian Healy managed well enough without one in 1989 Texaco game (6)
17. Fielders should give incoming batsman a dose of this (4)
19. Princess who should support Glamorgan (2)
20. Nickname of Navjot Sidhu's favourite bowler (5)
21. Nickname of balding English commentator, now resident in Oz (7)

Down

Solution on page 61

1. England's unfairly maligned strategy for retaining Ashes in 1930-31 (8)
2. Disastrous tourist to West Indies (see 12 across for namesake) (6)
3. Abid, Liaquat or Basit (3)
4. Geoffrey dropped at least one in India (6)
5. Nickname of the blunt Pudsey-born selector (4)
6. TV series not unlike England's tour of India (8)
8. Where journos watch the cricket team from (3)
10. He and Moore made bats (4)
16. Don't do this to Chinese prawns in India (3)
18. Size of Harry Pilling's head (3)

Q&A

Q: Why are the Scots so crap at cricket? M Fenton, Poole

A: I don't know, but they certainly are. A Smedley, Tavistock

A: They're crap at football, so why should they be any good at cricket?
N Martins, St Albans

A: They're too stingy to pay for proper coaching. And running around in kilts, tossing the caber and eating all that haggis gives them no time to prepare for the rigorous demands of cricket at the highest level. W Naylor, Carlisle

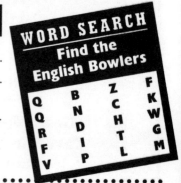

WORD SEARCH
Find the English Bowlers

58

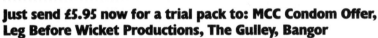

The men behind the microphones are familiar voices to us all but who is the 'voice of cricket' now that Johnners has gone to that great commentary box in the sky (not SKY, the real one).

By using the specially adapted Coopers and Lybrand software, *The Googly* has come up with the following commentator ratings and gives you this unique insight into the men in the commentary box.

Richie Benaud

Experience: Ex-Australian captain and over 250 test wickets
Employers: BBC TV, Channel 9 (Aus)
Obsessions: The incompetence of the world's cricket administrators, the front-foot no-ball law, the demise of the leg spinner
Virtues: Dry wit, penetrating analysis
Faults: Finds it impossible to have eye contact with his interviewer and always ends up peering beadily down the camera lens
Catchphrase: 'Morning everyone'

Rating 96

Tony Lewis

Experience: 9th choice captain to lead England to India in 1972-3 when nobody else could be bothered or didn't fancy the squits for six months
Employers: BBC TV, *Sunday Telegraph*
Obsessions: Lack of Welsh players in the England team
Virtues: Ability to 'anchor' coverage while wearing a monstrous bouffant toupee
Faults: Like Tony Blair, unable to talk without inane grin
Catchphrase: 'Hello and welcome to an overcast...' (insert appropriate test venue)

Rating 12

Geoff Boycott

Experience: Over 8,000 runs for England
Employers: BBC TV, BSkyB
Obsessions: Batting technique and 'kreeket' generally
Virtues: Deep technical knowledge
Faults: Excessive use of the magic marker on the screen and another grinner at the camera, only this time through a triangular-shaped mouth
Catchphrase: 'That's where a batsman hates it – the corridor of uncertainty'

Rating 28

Jack Bannister

Experience: Warwickshire trundler for donkey's years
Employers: BBC TV, *Birmingham Post*

Obsessions: The efficiency of the automated pitch cover at Edgbaston, the Brumbrella
Virtues: Soothing commentary, ideal for insomniacs
Faults: Breathes loudly through his nose down the microphone after each sentence
Catchphrase: 'What do you make of that, Geoffrey?'

Rating 5

Charles Colvile

Experience: Your guess is as good as ours
Employers: BSkyB
Obsessions: Winding Geoff Boycott up
Faults: Knows nothing about cricket
Virtues: Umm
Catchphrase: 'And he's gone !!!!!'
(forcing you to turn your volume control down)

Rating 1

Trevor Bailey

Experience: England 'all-rounder'
Employers: BBC Radio
Obsessions: Essex. He has been awarded the medal of the white sock for services rendered to his fellow Essex men by talking them up and into the test team
Virtues: Has put up with Fred Trueman for 20 years
Faults: Responsible for introducing horrid jargon – slip fielders have become 'slippers' and batsmen have become 'batters'
Catchphrase: 'He's not as good as Gooch/Stephenson/Such/Topley etc'

Rating 3

Fred Trueman

Experience: 67 tests
Employers: BBC Radio
Obsessions: Fred Trueman
Virtues: None
Faults: How long have you got?
Catchphrase: 'I just don't understand what's going on out there'. Or, 'If me, Les Jackson and Derek Shackleton had bowled on this pitch we'd have had 'em out for under 30'

Rating 0

CROSSWORD ANSWERS

Across

1 Botham, 4 Shine, 7 LB, 9 Day-night, 11 DA, 12 Taylor, 13 Loo, 14 Runner, 17 Clap, 19 Di, 20 Ernie, 21 Typhoon.

Down

1 Bodyline, 2 Taylor, 3 Ali, 4 Sitter, 5 Illy, 6 Eldorado, 8 Bar, 10 Gunn, 16 eat, 18 Pin.

Kent

Middlesex

NEW SUNDAY LEAGUE CRICKET STRIPS

Following on from the recent introduction of team colours for Sunday league games, we are pleased to announce that, for the 1995 season, a new range of county strips have been designed.

Derbyshire

Warwickshire

Yorkshire

Northamptonshire

Are YOU an old-fashioned FASCIST?

Find out in The Googly quiz

I. You hear Graham Gooch is retiring from test cricket. Is your reaction:

a Sadness. He's been a great batsman who has given enormous pleasure over the years.

b Anger. He's still the best opener in the world and should be encouraged to play at all costs.

c Relief. No wonder England played badly when the captain's a whining Essex secondary-modern, shell-suited oik with a ridiculous moustache and no university education.

••••••••••••••••••••••••••

2. You overhear Christopher Martin-Jenkins in a pub bemoaning the decline of the modern game. Do you:

a Walk over to him and tell him he's talking rubbish.

b Take him outside and attack his genitals with a baseball bat.

c Embrace him warmly crying 'Thank you! Thank you!' before kneeling before him and kissing his feet.

••••••••••••••••••••••••••

3. You read in the newspapers that coloured clothing is to be continued in the Sunday League next year. Do you:

a Applaud the initiative, recognising its clever marketing strategy of bringing more money into the game.

b Reflect on the sad but necessary need to make the game more commercial.

c Send a letter-bomb to the secretary of the TCCB and hire a hitman to assassinate the company directors of the clothing manufacturers.

••••••••••••••••••••••••••

4. You are at a Test match where peaceful demonstrators are objecting to the South African tour. Do you:

a Listen to their arguments.

b Become irritated by the noise.

c Listen to their ridiculous arguments, become irritated by the noise and disperse them by wielding

64

your shooting-stick in an offensive manner.

....

5. You have just finished watching a tape of England beating Australia for the Ashes in 1956. Do you:

a Feel good but reason that it's just a different game today.

b Feel good but reason that England will surely be as good again soon.

c Sob uncontrollably at the demise of our nation and ascribe it to socialism, the end of National Service and the advent of the permissive society.

....

HOW DID YOU DO?

....

Score: 5 pts for ⓐ, 10 pts for ⓑ, 20 pts for ⓒ

25-30 pts: Sorry. You're not old-fashioned at all. You're free-thinking, progressive and modern. Try to spend a bit more time with people who went to public schools.

31-50 pts: Not bad, but you're caught between two stools at the moment. Time to make a decision between the pinko values and the sort of principles that made Britain great.

51-100 pts: Well done, you old buffer! You're a dyed-in-the-wool fascist! Congratulate yourself by goose-stepping round the kitchen in your MCC tie and toasting the memory of Douglas Jardine.

'Take him outside and attack his genitals with a baseball bat!'

Every village team has one, but it's sometimes tricky working out if *you're*

1. You arrive early at the ground. The skipper hands you the old team bat and asks you to lead a spot of fielding practice. Do you:

a. Accept and provide a perfectly judged series of drives, skiers and slip-catches before giving up the bat to a team-mate?

b. Accept reluctantly and embarrass yourself when your shots fail to reach any of the fielders?

c. Refuse point blank – it's far too much effort for a fatty like you?

2. The batting order is being passed round. You're down at number 9 for the third week running. Do you:

a. Smile ruefully, shrug and offer to score for the first 20 overs?

b. Accept his decision, but suggest to the captain that when it comes to bowling he might need your leg-spin?

c. Mutter 'You stupid little git', tear up the list, pad up in the normal opener's kit and walk bandy-legged towards the square with a cry of 'You can face!' to your partner?

66

FAT OLD GIT?

3. It's your strike. The ball comes off your pad and your partner, already halfway down the wicket, calls for a suicidal single as cover point picks up the ball and shies at the bowler's end. Do you?

a. Take off immediately and, with an amazing burst of speed, manage to ground your bat at the non-striker's end before the bowler whips off the bails?

b. Think for a split second, realize that your partner, for all his hot-headed impatience, is by far the better bat, and trot two paces down the wicket so that it's you and not he that's run out?

c. You realize that someone's going to be run out (and it's certainly not going to be you) stand your ground, look your partner in the eye and shout 'Looks like you're out, you great prat!'

4. Your team takes the field. The skipper offers you:

a. Cover point. You know you're the sharpest fielder in the team. You accept willingly.

b. Fine leg. Ah well, you reflect, at least the exercise will do me good.

c. Fine leg. You refuse. 'Pulled a hamstring – I'll take first slip,' you shout. This allows you to stand still throughout the innings, legs slightly apart, hands on hips, a pipe or cigar clasped between your teeth, enjoying the gentle breeze riffling through your crotch. The only time you touch a moving ball is when the keeper tosses it to you after the batsman has played and missed.

6. It's after the match. You're standing naked in the changing room. Look straight down. What do you see?

a. Your todger and then your feet.

b. A gently wobbling mound of blubber, topped with curly mustard-coloured hair. Your feet are not visible, let alone your todger, but the unmistakable smell of ageing Cambozola confirms that they're down there somewhere.

c. Your chin.

How did you score?

Question (a) I point (b) 3 points (c) 5 points

The verdict

0-10 points. Well, softy, you're a likeable sort of chap, but you'll have to start asserting yourself a little more if you don't want to be pushed around by the fat old gits in the team.

10-20 points. So you think you're God's gift to cricket do you? Give it a few more years and you too could become a fat old git.

20-30 points. Hello Fatso! Congratulations! You are without doubt a fat old git. If you don't feel fully confident in the role, don't worry: fat old gits can only get fatter and older.

Alan Igglesden's

Health Page

? A fortnight ago, whilst in bed, I felt a slight twinge in the back. It hasn't hurt since, but do you think I should get it checked out? (Mr A Walker, Cardiff)

You really can't be too careful with back pain – especially a serious one like this. You should lie immobile on a hard surface for at least six weeks, and for a year afterwards avoid any strenuous activity. Like cricket for example.

....

? I am an athlete, and have recently developed an itch between my toes. On my foot, that is. And I'm an athlete. What could this be? (Ms C Shelford, Bucks)

I don't want to worry you, but itching or tingling in the extremities is a sure sign of spinal damage. Lie immobile for six weeks and I'm afraid you'll have to give up athletics for good.

....

? I've been picked for my school football team, in the semi-final of the local cup, and I've been losing sleep worrying about

it. **Do you think I should try sleeping tablets? (J Allen age 13, Suffolk)**

Ooh, it makes my back ache just thinking about it. That much tension could cause a stress fracture or worse. For big occasions like this, I'd recommend the *Modern Home Health Encyclopaedia* (1,300 pp, Methuen). It contains no useful information but if you drop it on your foot you should be able to break something and get out of the game.

....

? My family are considering the AA's health insurance policy – what do you think? (Mr D Lee, Eire)

Couldn't tell you mate – they refused me membership because I break down too often.

....

? My head hurts. I've got a migraine and I think I've been in the sun too long. (Mr C Lewis, Notts)

Oh, shut up and get out there you bleeding hypochondriac.

YOU ARE THE UMPIRE

1. The side batting first slump from 159 for 0 to 161 all out.

2. You inspect the ball. It looks as if it's been tampered with.

3. You notice bottle tops behind the stumps.

Do you...?

a Do nothing. It's normal for a ball to swing violently when it's 60 overs old.

b Tell the match referee your suspicions and let him sort it out.

c Sell your story to a tabloid newspaper saying the Pakistani captain is a cheat.

The answer is, of course:

d Replace the ball with another one, don't give the reason why and leave the matter unresolved so that rumour and speculation can thrive.

YOU are the third umpire

There is a close run out decision in an important match. The fielders all appeal. The umpire calls you on his walkie-talkie to ask for a ruling.

Do you... ?

a Look at the replay and curse the BBC for giving you such hopeless pictures.

b Delay your decision until 'Neighbours' is finished.

c Take a vote in the bar.

Answer:

It depends on which team you want to win.
If it's the batting side, then he's not out.
If it's the bowling side, he's out.

FACT F·I·L·E

Duckwatch

DUCK IN FIRST TEST INNINGS

B P Julian (A)

G D McGrath (A)

I R Bishop (WI)

C Kuggelijn (NZ) **PAIR**

D K Morrison (NZ)

N H Fairbrother (E)

C J Richards (E)

N V Radford (E)

J G Thomas (E)

M G Hughes (A)

S P O'Donnell (A)

K Rutherford (NZ) **PAIR**

Wasim Akram (P)

C J McDermott (A)

R A Harper (WI)

R B Richardson (WI)

C L Smith (E)

K Srikkanth (I)

P W G Parker (E)

M R Whitney (A)

M D Marshall (WI)

B A Edgar (NZ)
B P Bracewell (NZ) **SAME INNINGS**

G A Cope (E)

G D Barlow (E)

G B Troup (NZ)

J M Brearley (E)
H A Gomes (WI) **SAME MATCH**

G A Gooch **PAIR**

Reverse Swing

Reginald Dwight, professor of Aerodynamics at the University of Littlehampton, explains why swinging both ways is the most natural thing in the world.

Over the past couple of years I have carried out a series of controlled wind-tunnel experiments which demonstrate not only the mechanics of how swing arises in a cricket ball, but also how the mysterious reverse swing, so recently arrived on these shores, comes into existence.

1 Perfect sphere

Here we see the flow over the sphere's surface is a smooth flow until a certain point at which the boundary layer separates and turbulence is created. As this occurs at the same point on each half of the sphere, no swing arises.

2 Normal swing

Here the flow on the dull side of the ball becomes turbulent very quickly due to the action of the seam whereas the boundary layer stays intact much longer on the other side of the ball, aided by the shine. The imbalance creates the swing force.

3 Reverse swing

The flow on the dull side of the ball is as in 2 above. However, as we can see, the flow over the shiny side quickly becomes highly turbulent due to the presence of a Newcastle Brown Ale bottle cap which has been embedded in the ball. This causes a net lateral force which produces movement at 180 degrees to that in 2.

Next issue – six astrologers attempt to explain the England selection process.

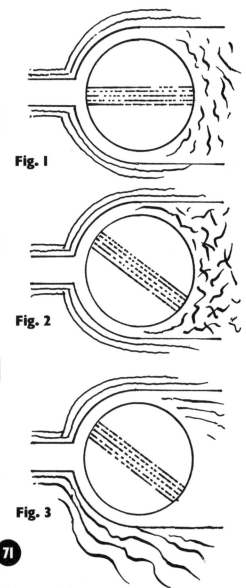

Fig. 1

Fig. 2

Fig. 3

Colvile's

T I P S

Sky presenter Charles Colvile gives his tips to would-be commentators on how to make it to the top

1

Smart haircut. I find that it helps me look good on TV and gives me the confidence to give that little bit extra.

2

Smart blazer. Every commentator should have one. I feel Michael Holding sets a bad example with his open necked shirt - he still has a lot to learn.

3

No knowledge of cricket. It certainly hasn't held me back. Jack Bannister agrees with me on this point.

4

No talent for playing cricket. Again Jack and I see eye-to-eye on this. Those who can, do; those who can't, commentate; those who can't commentate, end up on Sky.

5

Public-school smugness. A certain aloofness helps in dealing with our Commonwealth cousins and Englishmen from Essex.

ENGLAND'S HEAVYWEIGHT XI

Neil Taylor (Kent)
15 stone

David Smith (Sussex)
16.0

Mike Gatting (Middx)
15.7

Ian Botham (Durham)
15.5

Martin Weston (Worcs)
15.7

Derek Pringle (Essex)
16.7

Robert Turner (Somerset)
13.8 (wkt)

Martin McCague (Kent)
15.10

Angus Fraser (Middx)
15.7

Gary Wigham (Durham)
16.7

David Lawrence (Gloucs)
16.7

12th man

Devon Malcolm (Derby)
15.6

Jack Russell's GALLERY

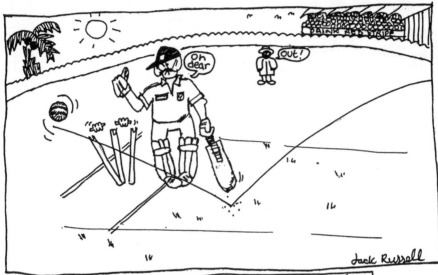

"ME PLAYING IN THE WEST INDIES" 1994

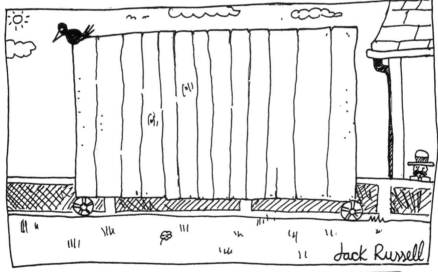

"BLACK BIRD ON WHITE SIGHTSCREEN"
(bit arty this one)   1992

THE Mike Gatting Cook

All cricketers have big appetites. The combination of hard graft in the field and long periods on the road means that the lads like to work hard and play hard. Some of the guys like a beer or two. Others have a soft spot for the ladies. A few may even pass the time puffing on a crack pipe. As for me, well I like the occasional spot of dinner. After a day laying willow on to leather, there's nothing more pleasant than the sound of EPNS on china. The fellows rib me now and then about my eating, but I still feel as lithe and trim as ever. So here's a few of my favourite recipes just for you.

Potage avec le pain blanc

I uncut white loaf

I tin soup

butter

salt and pepper

Tear a slice off the end of the loaf. Pull the insides out. Pour in the hot soup. Push bits of bread back in to soak up the soup. Top off with a nob (1 lb) butter. Salt and pepper to taste. Put on plastic mac then eat with gusto.

Chocolate sandwich

2 x 2lb bars Cadbury's Milk

I jar chocolate spread

butter

Unwrap the choc-choc. Smear the smooth sides with butter then add generous dollops of chocolate spread. Form a sandwich with the two slabs. Eat as if you'll never eat another meal again.

Crispy chicken tikka

4 X Marks and Spencer Family Size Heat 'n' Serve Chicken Tikkas

I pint cream

I jar mango chutney

I economy size box of corn flakes

Pour the heated chicken tikkas into a bucket. Ladle the cream over the meat. Sprinkle liberally with corn flakes and top off with several spoonfuls of mango chutney. Eat with trowel, reminding

book

your friends to watch their fingers should they get too near your mouth.

Kebab a la Gatt

1 doner kebab (the whole lot, rotating on a skewer)

1 bottle tomato ketchup

Kneel on floor in front of rotating kebab. Using a chainsaw, slice huge chunks of meat off the kebab. As they fall, catch the chunks in your mouth. Squirt in tomato ketchup to taste. Make huge slurping noises as you eat.

Mike's cow pie

1 boned cow

14 tins of Bisto gravy granules

2 gallons water

1 duvet-sized slab of puff pastry

Put cow in bath. Cover with gravy granules. Shower in the water. Slap on the pastry. Cook for one hour in industrial microwave. Enjoy.
Serves 1 (me). Eat in the manner of a hyena chomping on a gazelle.

PEOPLE I HATE

by Geoff Boycott

Brian Close

Great player, great captain, complete bastard. Got me sacked by Yorkshire in 1986.

Ray Illingworth

Splendid all rounder, wily skipper, utter tosser. Got me sacked as Yorkshire captain in 1979.

Fred Trueman

Superb fast bowler, wonderful character, absolute prat. Tried to get me sacked by Yorkshire for 20 years.

Keith Fletcher

Cunning leader, nifty batter, total prick. Got me sacked from the England tour of India in 1982.

Umpires respond to intimidatory appealing

Cricket

A Beginner's Guide

THE GOOGLY tackles the questions most often asked by people new to our wonderful game

Q What do the men in the white coats do?

A The ones in the middle are the umpires. The ones on the boundary with the big net are just looking after Phil Tufnell.

Q Why don't the bowlers just throw it instead?

A A good question. There are a couple of Sri Lankan spinners who haven't figured that one out yet.

Q Why do they rub the ball on their trousers?

A Are you kidding? A hand-stitched, high-seam Reader ball has been described as 'better than sheep' by one Glamorgan quickie.

Q What about swing then? Something about non-linear hydrodynamic flow or something isn't it?

A Christ knows. Ask me another one.

Q Why don't they use a softer ball – the hard one is dangerous!

A More and more cricketers agree – Chris Lewis, for example, always lets the batsmen

A They are Andy Caddick and Alan Igglesden, and there's no need to get personal.

Q What is a googly?

A Depends. If you're a TV commentator, it's a leg break that fails to turn. If you're a batsman, it's any delivery from a leg spinner which bowls you. And if you're Ian Salisbury, it's four.

Q I've often heard them say 'The heavy roller was in action during the lunch interval'. What does that mean?

A Oh, that's just Ian Botham enjoying himself.

smash the ball into a spongey mess before he tries to bowl quick.

Q Why do they all wear white?

A Er, they don't any more actually.

Q Why do they all clap their opponents?

A Er, they don't any more actually.

Q Why do England win all the time?

A Are you taking the piss or something?

Q Sorry. What are those big white squares at

Q Why did they keep dropping David Gower?

A Um ... ask me that one about hydrodynamic flow again ...

It's Sunday. It's summer. You're hoping to have a lie-in and you're dreaming that your partner gets up especially early to make breakfast for you before washing the car, cleaning the house and mending the clothes rail in your wardrobe that he's been promising to fix for seven months.

Perhaps he even brings you the Sunday papers and, after a warm and lengthy session of lovemaking, he takes you out for a romantic stroll in the country followed by lunch at a quiet restaurant. That's what you're dreaming.

What you actually get is your partner crawling around the bedroom in his skiddies, shouting at you to get up and help him find his white trousers. The pair he gets out once a year for the annual cricket match.

For this is the Once-a-Year Cricketer.

The Once

How to spot the Once-a-Year Cricketer

The OYC (pronounced 'oik') is not a regular player. He is neither good enough nor interested enough to join a team. He will, however, play once a year with 'me mates' to 'keep me hand in'. So, at about the same time every summer, he pulls on the slightly flared cream trousers he used to wear for best on Saturday nights down Cinderella's, does them up with the help of a large safety pin and turns into Graham Gooch about to take on the West Indies at Sabina Park.

The OYC is a cricket expert. You know this because he watches one day matches on the telly and shouts instructions to the England team: 'Play with a straight bat, you *nonce*, Rampers, get yer feet *moving*.'

'Salisbury, you *spanner!* Pitch it in *the rough*.'

'Is that *any bloody way* to bring on a drinks trolley?'

'Pathetic. Look at that pile of sawdust; it's nowhere near big enough.'

And so on.

The OYC may have played the odd game at school. He fondly remembers the time he took a wicket and scored a dozen runs. This adds to his air of expertise and he will tell you that 'once it's in your blood, you never forget how to play.'

The partner of an OYC is expected to:

Ⓐ share his excitement at playing

Ⓑ make the sandwiches for tea, and

a-Year Cricketer

C cart him home after closing time when he will be so drunk he could probably puke for England.

The OYC wears Dunlop Green Flash or Clark's Polyvelds.

The OYC plays on pitches that double as dog toilets. If it has not rained just before his game, it will do soon.

Their partners will no doubt find themselves sheltering under a sodden *Sunday Telegraph* Review Section while the OYC, so wet that his red and grey under-pants can now be clearly seen through his trousers, declares that 'it's only just spitting. He'll get out in a minute.'

If the rain stops, as it sometimes does during an English summer, play commences – but not before:

A several players from one team join the other in order to even out the numbers

B one player is sick in the equipment bag (a carrier with two stumps and a child-size bat in it)

C fights break out over what to use for the toss, who'll do the umpiring, who'll keep the score, how many overs to play, and why no one remembered to bring any decent equipment.

The game can then begin.

Partners of the OYCs see this as a cue to make the sandwiches, as it is less tedious than watching the match.

The following rules apply when an OYC plays:

A When the ball is thrown to you, you drop it.

B When you throw the ball to someone else, you miss them completely.

C When you bat, you get out almost immediately without troubling the scorer.

D When you bowl, you bring a whole new meaning to the word 'scattergun'.

E If the ball is hit to you in the air, it will sail through your hands.

F If the ball is hit along the ground, it will fly through your legs.

G When you try to make a catch, you will invariably slip on a turd, land on your backside and skid over the boundary, through the kiddies' playground and out into the car park.

The OYC will be out for nought, probably first ball, and return bowling figures of 1-0 - 40 - 0, with five wides, four no-balls and a ten-minute delay while the square leg fielder recovers from being hit on the side of the head by a beamer.

The OYC will lose the match but declare the proceedings 'brilliant, anyone for a pint?'

The OYC bears an uncanny resemblance to several players in the England squad.

The Googly's Book Review

The winter months see the publication of a number of cricket books to keep the cricket fan amused through those cold, dark nights. Here's a selection of those you might have missed.

■ Ooh, Lanky! Lanky!

The Lancashire CCC supporters' song book with such evergreen favourites as 'Lancashire la la la, Lancashire la la la,' and 'Oh, Lanky, Lanky, Lanky, Lanky, Lanky, Lankyshire!" Cassette also available.

■ Life's a Pitch

Harry Brind's hilarious account of the relaying of the Oval square in 1985.

■ Boycott on Boycott

Geoff talks about his favourite subject and asks himself the question: What made me the genius I was? Volumes 1, 2, 3 for £29.99.

■ Jung, Freud and Wicketkeepers

By Mike Brearley. Ex-England captain and latterday psychoanalyst examines the sexual habits of the world's glovemen and probes their potty training.

■ Shep

Umpire David Shepherd's pop-up book of umpiring hand signals, including his famous Nelson hopping routine.

■ Take Cover!

Foreword by Jack Bannister. A picture book of Edgbaston's Brumbrella. Over 140 photographs of the pioneering pitch cover combating the Birmingham drizzle.

■ Bill Frindall's Wisdens

The eminent cricket statistician takes us on a vivid tour of his favourite pages of over 120 Wisden Cricket Almanacks. For example, page 27 in the 1931 Almanack, the first page to carry an advert and page 496 of the 1956 Almanack — Jim Laker's 19-90, the most thumbed page in the Wisden Library. A must for any retarded statistician.

■ Who Killed Wendy Wimbush?

A cricketing thriller written by ageing boy racer and ex-chairman of selectors, Ted Dexter, and his brother Colin, the man behind Inspector Morse.

THE DISCOVERY OF FIRE

LIFELINES:

Shane Warner

Who is the closest person to you?

Right now? Well, the chalet maid in the other room, I guess.

Where and when were you happiest?

When my mates first saw my peroxide job, and got 'Wanker' tattooed on my butt. I knew then that I really belonged.

Who was the biggest influence on your cricketing career?

My old scoutmaster. When I was 12 he suggested I try different grips and wrist positions. And he said I'd look nice with blond hair too.

Who or what is the love of your life?

Steak and chips.

What is your favourite food?

My girlfriend Shanice.

Who do you most admire in cricket?

My old team-mate Peter Heather. One time he was sledging this batsman from short leg, and anyway the guy lost his concentration and Peter caught him. He then spat on the guy as he was walking off, and called him a 'f—— useless c——'. After the match he picked a fight with the guy and beat him to a pulp - total cricket!

Who is your favourite author?

Geoff Stevenson. He wrote this real good book, *Shane Warner, the Official Biography*. It's a hysterical novel about some jerk who thinks he's the bee's knees but all his mates secretly hate his guts.

What was your greatest cricketing triumph?

No question – the second day of Victoria v Queensland on 15 November 1991 was a day I'll never forget. I won a $100 bet with Dale Carter when he collapsed after 22 pints of lager. Mind you, he never actually paid up – he unluckily choked to death on his own vomit. His family didn't want to pay up either but I went along to the funeral and insisted.

What is your dream car?

Mazda MX5 turbo. The soft-top estate version with the optional mattress.

What is your motto in life?

'Give everyone the respect you would wish for yourself.' Oh, and 'You can't bat you f——g pommie w——r.'

Atherton

1 At 13, Michael is England's youngest captain since the turn of the century when W G Grace led a victorious England XI to Australia in beard and diapers at the tender age of six months.

MY KIND OF DAY

by Bill Frindall

I normally wake up between 7 and 7.30. In fact, over the last 14 years my average wake up time is 7.19. Much better than my wife, whose sleeping patterns vary enormously. On 24 March 1986, she woke up at a staggering 4.12 am to put the cat out, which in fact is the earliest time the cat has been put out for a pee in 8 years... (not to be continued).

2 Like Mike Brearley, the last England captain to have an O level, Atherton is a chess grand master, a philosophy don and a card-carrying Roman Catholic archdeacon.

3 Mike likes to be called 'smartarse' by his team-mates.

4 Michael's mum knows Mark Lathwell's mum and both of them think their offspring should have become accountants.

5 Michael was fined £400,000 by ICC referee Peter Burge for not snogging the umpire on being given out.

6 At Cambridge, Michael astonished his team-mates by chairing a seminar on Early English Agricultural Collectives while compiling a respectable half-century for the varsity against Northants.

7 Mikey has arranged the Lancashire county song ('Oh, Lanky, Lanky,

facts

Durham
CRICKET CLUB'S
MANIFESTO

bout England's skipper ●

Lanky, Lanky, Lanky, Lanky, Lanky-shire') for string orchestra.

8 Mike possesses neither pink-framed sunglasses nor white 'total block' lip-protector. He considers such accoutrements of the modern game to be 'common'.

9 Michael has recently signed an exclusive multi-million-pound sponsorship deal with the Alexandra Hospital, Cheadle, under the terms of which, should he be killed during a Test Match, his brain will be transplanted by a skilled team of surgeons into the head of Alec Stewart.

10 Mike likes to grow tomatoes in his trousers.

1 We will lose as many matches as possible

2 We will employ as many washed-out second-rate players as possible

3 We will maximize Dean Jones's talent by making him 2nd XI coach

4 We will play our matches on Durham University's playing fields

MIKE ATHERTON'S GUIDE TO

Fielding Positions

I. Wicketkeeper

This position traditionally goes to one of two types – either the bloke in your team who has bought all the kit including the keeper's gloves and won't let anybody else use it, or some nutter who can't sit still, can't stop fidgeting and has the attention span of a lobotomized goldfish unless involved all the time.

2. First slip

The favoured resting ground of your oldest, fattest, laziest player. Note where Mike Gatting fields for Middlesex.

3. Second slip

Often patrolled by the nerd wearing glasses who can't throw and has the reflexes of a slug on sedatives or worse, Graeme Hick.

4. Third man

Put your temperamental fast bowler down here out of the way. Let him brood and develop a psychotic hatred of the batsman. In his day John Snow would attack the crowd when his dander was up.

5. Gully

This fielder has to deal with rasping square cuts. Put your occasional spin bowler who is always pestering you to let him purvey his chinamen heavily disguised as full tosses, here. With luck, he'll pick up a hand injury. I like to use Ian Salisbury here.

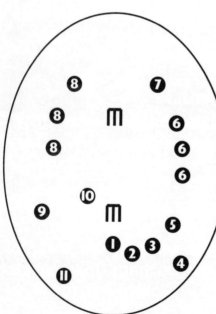

6. Point, cover, extra-cover

The athletic young nippers who are still at school should patrol the vast expanse of the covers. Let them do all the running about and thrashing about in the bushes looking for balls. When it comes to bat, they'll be next to useless, so make use of their legs now. Ramprakash was my man for the covers in the Caribbean.

7. Mid-off

The captain's position - here you can offer encouraging words like 'try getting the ball to bounce, Salisbury' or pass on tactical titbits to your bowlers, like 'you see those three sticks, Devon? Try aiming at those and not third slip's kneecap.' You can also smear the ball with dirt without being noticed.

8. Mid-on, midwicket

In club cricket this is where the catches go. In Test cricket you put your biggest donkey here. Pringle, Fraser and Igglesden have all done sterling service for England here.

9. Square leg

Station your most inarticulate, socially inept player here. You don't want him nattering to the umpire all day. Bill Athey would be my ideal choice.

10. Short leg

Who is your club arsehole? You know the one – he's got all the kit but can't play for toffee. He's a desperate bore down the pub, he set fire to his Hawaiian shirt at the club barbecue and spends his sad, pathetic life bowling in the back garden to his three-year-old son 'trying to perfect his flipper'. Well here's your chance to do the whole club a big favour and give team

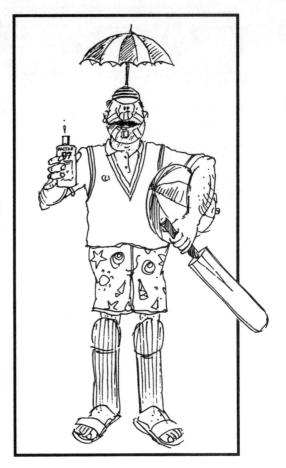

morale a welcome boost. Bung him here and wait for him to get one full on the frontal lobe. He won't mind. In fact, such an arsehole will think he's being afforded special status.

II Fine leg

Just the place for the vice-captain or that pushy heir apparent. Keep them well away from the action. You can do without them putting their oar in and coming up with bright ideas that show you up. Just the place for Stewie.

It's important to get your fielders in the right place but that's easier said than done with Devon, Tuffers, Gus and Iggy in your team. Good luck!

85

MY TV DINNER

David Shepherd

My favourite TV shows are 'Cannon', 'French and Saunders' and anything with Robbie Coltrane.

I like to watch with my dinner on a tray and my perfect meal would be the following:

One cow

One skipful of potatoes

Two lorryloads of carrots

One season's crop of sweetcorn from the State of Tennessee

A couple of EC butter mountains

Ian Botham's wine cellar

A seven-ton ice cream (like the one made by the children of Ormskirk Primary School for Record Breakers in 1986)

Desert Island  DISCS

If cast away on an island — say, somewhere in the West Indies — which records would you take with you? This week, England selector Keith Fletcher makes his choice.

1 That one by little Jimmy Osmond would be my first choice, I think. He's only young but he's going to be very, very good one day. You have to invest in youth, you know.

2 Anything by Stevie Wonder. He's an inspiration to us all, doing his job with absolutely no vision whatsoever.

3 'Agadoo' by Black Lace. Quality just speaks for itself, doesn't it?

4 A Smiths single — they were renowned for having dodgy A-sides, weren't they? I think that's something I can relate to.

5 Hmm. I know — a frisbee! If you get the ones with a grooved top, you can use them as a sort of record as well, as they're kind of good all-round choice.

6 Er ... The Guinness Book of Records? Cheating I suppose, but it's got lots of records in it, so I'd never be short of music.

7 Neil Foster. Sorry, I always write that when I run out of ideas. OK, that's my last choice.

And finally, what luxury would you like to take to the West Indies with you?

'What, apart from Ian Salisbury you mean?'

'I wouldn't exactly call it a batsman's wicket'

"I'm shit" says Lara

Brian Lara, Warwickshire's record-breaking West Indian batsman, yesterday admitted that he was 'shit'.

Speaking after his 653 not out against Essex broke the record for the highest score in any form of cricket, the little left-hander said 'This does not mean that I am a great batsman. In fact, I think I'm shit.

'Comparing me to Bradman is a joke,' he went on, 'there are better players in this Warwickshire team than me. Roger Twose, for one, has far more talent. So does Trevor Penney. And when Andy Moles gets fit I might struggle to get in the side.'

The ever-modest Lara said he was amazed at all the sponsorship deals he was being offered. 'I really am not very good, you know. When I see someone like Asif Din batting I think to myself: I wish that was me.'

OBITUARIES

Burk, Kenneth

who died 1 April 1993, aged 67, was President of Little Muke CC in north Surrey and had played for the club for 40 years. He went out to bat at no 11 for the club second XI against Surbiton, hit a six and then was killed by a bouncer next ball.

Van Gross, Corrie

died on 18 March 1993, aged 87. Corrie van Gross played two cup matches for Orange Free State in 1929-30 against Transvaal and Natal. He scored 0,0,0 and 0. He did not take a catch in either of the games. Free State lost by an innings and 405 and an innings and 207.

Ajit Vambli

who died on 9 November 1992, was one of the least competent Test umpires India ever had. He was relentlessly one-sided in favour of the Indian team and it comes as no surprise that he was found poisoned in his hotel room while on holiday in Pakistan.

Van Gogh, Vincent

who took his own life on 6 March 1993, was a cricketing perfectionist not unlike his namesake, the fine Dutch painter. Unable to convince the selectors that he was the best bowler in Holland, he cut his ear off and then shot himself when the bowler chosen in his place took a hat-trick.

Seventh Devon

Hick's Duncan Fearnley 405, Goochie's SS 333? Forget them. For the real batting experience, use Devon Malcolm's DEV 26 (remember his vintage knock of 26 against the Minor Counties last year?)

The bat has no middle to lure bowlers into thinking the batsman's timing is off. But its edges are specially reinforced, so practise nicking the ball and watch the boundaries flow the Devon Malcolm way.

Chris Lewis Joins The Chippendales

As the season draws to an end, county pros all over the country are making plans for the winter months ahead. We know who is going to Australia and who is off on the A tour, while a number of others will be off to play grade cricket in Australia (*Mike Garnham*), coaching in South Africa (*Bill Athey*) or even going back to school (*Nick Folland*).

But for some of the stars of county cricket it's a tough life in the winter. We sent our award-winning investigative journalists off to find out just what some of the game's giants will be up to these cold, dark months.

Blubbery

It's a bleak time ahead for Lancashire's rotund trundler, *Ian Austin*. He pays the bills as a grossagram exposing his blubbery body to any office party which can cough up a ten-ner. 'If *Chris Lewis* can do it why can't I?' says the fat seamer. But things are

THE SAMARITANS

'It's Keith Fletcher again.'

• DAVID HOLLAND •

worse for Surrey batsman, David Ward, who is going into training with Lambourn-based Jenny Pitman with the Grand National as his long-range target.

Show business is one field where cricketers are finding more opportunities ever since Ian Botham donned the tights in panto. This year Neil Mallender has found part-time work in a fun fair haunted house, Chris Lewis is joining the Chippendales, Graham Gooch is to play a Mexican bandit in a new Spaghetti Western called 'A Fistful of Krugerrands' and Mike Gatting is playing the part of a ewe in labour in BBC TV's 'All Creatures Great and Small'.

Balls

The winter will be like any other for Eddie Hemmings – a spot of bingo, a run out in the car when his grandchildren come to visit and a diet of meals on wheels, while Durham batsman John Morris has decided to quit the game and has joined Australian airline Quantas.

But for some of the other players it is very much business as usual. David Gower will commentate on the exploits of lesser mortals down under. Alan Igglesden will be on the physio's couch, and Graeme Hick will be removing cricket balls from the grill of his helmet.

The MCC gets back to basics

MCC FLOGS MEMBERS

MCC members seen participating in the 'Mexican Wave' during the recent Lord's test were flogged, it was revealed yesterday.

'They were clearly enjoying themselves,' said MCC Secretary Tim Lamb, 'so they had to be punished.'

The offenders were stripped and covered in linseed oil before receiving thirty strokes with the cat o' nine tails, administered by Lamb himself.

Any future incidents of MCC members indulging in what Lamb called 'fun' would be dealt with even more ruthlessly.

'In future,' he said, 'we will stone them with bails in the Long Room and then crucify them on Old Father Time.'

Well, this is the life! First session of the first day. 12.58 and Dave and Nick look like they'll see us through 'til lunch. Might as well start taking the pads off ... Oh my God, Dave's out!

Oh no! Where are my gloves? God, Dave, you prat ... Down the steps. Look nonchalant but competent. Don't trip you'll look stupid and don't catch anyone's eye. I hate it when the members stare at you ... look at that old buffer. He's never clapped me in once ... right ... swing the bat. Loosen the shoulders ... what does that Allan Border do? Stare at the sky ... yeah ... Ow! Bit bloody bright isn't it? Should've brought my sponsored sunglasses. Okay – here comes Dave – try to look as if you're not blaming him – prat.

Right then ... 'Middle and off, please umpire.' Silly old duffer. You're the old

Inside the Head of your County Batsman

fool who gave me out leg before playing half a mile forward last season ... time to get the legendary concentration going ... survey the scene ... check the field ... I wonder what's for lunch today? Stop it. Concentrate ... better ring mum this evening ... concentrate. Concentrate! ... Hello, that bloke at gully looks just like ... What's his name ... come on, the scientist ... flaps his arms like Magnus Pike! Yes. Magnus ... oh for God's sake concentrate!!! Right then ... what have we got? A nice bit of spin? No ... too long a run up. Swing then ...? Who is this bloke? Matthew something I think they called him ... makes you wish you'd watched a bit more of the game, times like this. I don't believe it ... he's still walking back. Oh my God he's quick! Of course he's quick – he got Dave out last over before lunch. They were banging the middle stump in when I got here ... The keeper had to practically bring the bails back from the boundary. Oh my God! He is still walking back! Keep calm. Don't panic. Front foot – that's the way to handle these flash kids. Punching demoralizing fours through the covers. Four, four, four ... that'll teach the young ... Oh my God! He's turning! Just keep it out you fool! Don't panic! ... Here he comes! He'll probably welcome me with a short one! I'll cut it majestically down to third man. No! Wait ... I'll pull it. No I won't I'll come down the pitch and drive it back over his head! No pull it. No ... block ... no ... cut ... pull ... cut ... Here it is ... HOOK!

(Silence)

That was close. Half a centimetre nearer the bat and I'd have edged it.

Well ... three more balls to lunch ... who says we modern batsmen can't handle the four-day game?!

The Googly
T·E·C·H·N·O·L·O·G·Y
Page

The television presentation of cricket has improved in leaps and bounds over the last few years. Some of us can still remember the days when Brian Johnston used to sit in front of what looked like an old box of Frosties painted green by Valerie Singleton with a Fuzzy Felt cricket figure glued to it.

Then there were the TV lights shining brightly on Peter West's spartan dome as he introduced coverage that during alternate overs consisted of a prime view of Alan Knott's clenched buttocks and very little else.

But the Packer revolution has brought with it all kinds of presentation advances; cameras at both ends of the ground, graphics that you can read, and slow motion replays that no longer look like a repeat of the action you've just seen only this time in an Arctic blizzard.

Sound engineers have also done their bit especially those in the sound dept at Channel 9 in Australia. The Aussie TV bosses felt viewers were not close enough to the action. They wanted us to hear the grunts and groans of battle.

First, they tried secreting special effects microphones about the umpire's person but this was abandoned following a bizarre accident involving Dickie Bird, who confused his miniature battery cell microphone with a sennapod and had to have it surgically removed in a Sharjah hospital.

Instead they turned to sound effects rather than sound recording. They discovered that by ripping a piece of Velcro close to a microphone they could simulate the sound of an approaching bowler in his delivery stride. So now, every ball, we hear the man with the Velcro ripping away.

But the big breakthrough has to be the stump-view camera affording viewers a fantastic view of the batsman's feet. Excellent for showing whether the batsman has done his shoelaces up or whether or not he's wearing spikes or 'slippers' (as Ray Illingworth would have it).

And that is just the start of it. This season will see trial use of the 'box' camera. Located within the abdominal protector of the batsman, the camera is designed to attract female viewers to the game. With the West Indies touring in 1995, this particular view of cricket is sure to be a success with the girls (see below).

View from the box camera

MY DreamTeam

by Kepler Wessels

**Flexibility is the key word to my team
and I've gone for players who can play for any country:**

(1) Kepler Wessels
South Africa, Australia, South Africa

(2) Younis Ahmed
Pakistan, qualified for England, Pakistan

(3) Graeme Hick
Zimbabwe and England

(4) Monte Lynch
England (one-day internationals) and West Indies (rebel tour)

(5) Craig White
Australia and England

(6) Nawab of Pataudi snr
England and India

(7) Dipak Patel
England and New Zealand

(8) Andy Caddick
New Zealand and England

(9) Martin McCague
Australia and New Zealand

(10) John Aldridge
England and Ireland

(11) Zola Budd
South Africa and Great Britain

Young Gentlemen Cricketers

ON THE 1994-5 WINTER TOUR TO AUSTRALIA

Stand tall and proud young men, for not only are you the cream of your nation's cricketing talent, but you also have the rare opportunity of acting as ambassadors for your country in the far-off continent of AUSTRALIA.

As such we know how keen you will be to put your best foot forward on all occasions, not just when approaching the popping crease.

Naturally we understand how exciting it can be to leave your native land for the first time. We also realize that many temptations await; the odd 'tinnie' can make one feel quite heady after a long day in the field!

In order to assist our youthful travellers make the very most of their trip, we are pleased to offer this brief guide.

An evening out in Brisbane

We recommend a quiet night with the local cricket representatives spent in conversation, perhaps al fresco, at the Hyatt. A chance to mingle and get to know your hosts, or even risk a quick foxtrot to The Bushwacker Didgeridoo Band.

We do not recommend scoring half a kilo of prime Thai stick cannabis, washing it down with five litres of Toohies, nicking a Hyundai jeep, driving downtown, bursting into a local bar and shouting 'Which one of you sheep molesters fancies a fight?'

A sunny afternoon in Melbourne

We can think of no better way to spend an afternoon off than to hike up to the cool, clear water of the Yarra River. On the way back why not stop at one of the many aboriginal craft centres to buy some small, hand-carved boomerang for loved ones back home?

Please do not sink seventeen bottles of Japanese whisky, hire a Harley and screech through Melbourne looking for some 'hot Aussie babe' whom you feel might enjoy 'a bit of the old Hampshire Ham Hatstand'.

At the British Embassy, Sydney

There is nothing finer than hearing the stories and enjoying the company of expatriates. Such gay and refined company, and so well educated. We are sure the local school's fifth-form string quartet will enrapture you with its unique interpretations of Bach, Handel and Rolf Harris.

What is not quite so clever is to cop two grammes of cocaine, snort it off the stomach of the ambassador's daughter, then leap naked into the hotel swimming pool with the cricket correspondent of the *Daily Telegraph*.

On returning home

After the Herculean efforts that have gone before, one must remember to always be on one's best behaviour, even down to the final moments of departure. If you must 'go wild', then why not spend a few pounds on a bottle of Australian Chardonnay in the local duty free shop then reflect on what you have learnt during the tour.

Try not to scout round for a decent bit of fluff who fancies a quick one in a nearby cupboard, particularly if everyone else is on board the aircarft and waiting to depart.

England in Australia

The TCCB has taken a firm stand with the Australian Cricket Board in agreeing the England tour itinerary of Australia in 1994–5 following criticism that players were being asked to play in too many games and doing too much travelling.

The full itinerary is as follows:

28 Nov. v **Qantas Baggage Handlers XI** (Perth)

29 Nov. v **Melbourne Cub Scouts** (Melbourne)

30 Nov. v **Perth Rotary Club** (Perth)

1-4 Dec. v **South Australia** (Adelaide)

5-9 Dec. v **Northern Territory** (Darwin)

10 Dec. v **Aboriginal XI** (Ayres Rock Picnic Area)

11 Dec. v **Western Australia** (Perth)

12 Dec. v **Australia** - First One Day International (Sydney)

13 Dec. v **Australia** - Second One Day International (Brisbane)

14 Dec. v **Australia** - Third One Day International (Adelaide)

15 Dec. v **Australia** - Fourth One Day International (Hobart)

16 Dec. v **Australia** - Fifth One Day International (Fiji)

17 Dec. v **Australia** - Sixth One Day International (Melbourne)

18 Dec. v **Australia** - Seventh One Day International (Adelaide)

19 Dec. v **Australia** - Eighth One Day International (Perth)

20-26 Dec. **1st Test v Australia** (Brisbane)

27 Dec. v **Australia** - Ninth One Day International (Melbourne)

etc etc etc

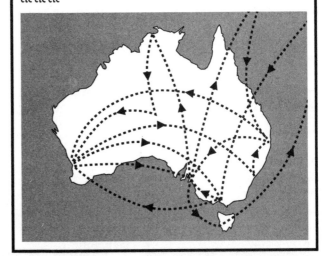

ARE YOU Jack Bannister?

1. A ball pitches two feet outside leg stump and misses off stump. Would you say:

a. 'That turned a mile.'
b. 'That turned a mile and a half.'
c. 'Just the slight suggestion of a turn there, Geoffrey.'

2. Atherton cuts the ball past point for four. Would you say:

a. 'Lovely shot.'
b. Nothing.
c. 'Atherton cuts the ball past point for four.'

3. Rain has stopped play. Do you:

a. Ask Geoffrey Boycott to sum up the play so far.
b. Return viewers back to Des Lynam in the Wimbledon studio.
c. Talk about the Brumbrella (Edgbaston's pitch cover) for half an hour.

Not as stupid a question as it looks. Of course, you know you're not but perhaps you're beginning to sound like him. Fill in our questionnaire and find out the truth.

The verdict

If you answered c to any of these questions, there is a greater than 90% chance that you are Jack Bannister. If you can add tweed jackets and dim memories of playing county cricket then I'm afraid the evidence is conclusive.

4. Who do you believe to be the most potent new ball bowling attack in the world?

a. Wasim and Waqar.
b. Ambrose and Walsh.
c. Munton and Reeve.

5. To win friends and get laughs at school, did you?

a. Develop comedy impressions of the teaching staff.
b. Practise elementary magic tricks.
c. Learn to speak whilst simultaneously breathing out of your nose.

6. Do you believe the end of the Cold War was achieved by?

a. Economic destabilisation of the Iron Curtain countries.
b. Domestic pressure for peace from the West.
c. Footwork.

"ADMIT IT REAPER .... YOU'VE BEEN APPLYING LIP-SALVE TO THE BALL, HAVEN'T YOU?"

CONGRATULATIONS!

YOU HAVE WON A MAJOR PRIZE!

YES, **Mr Graham Gooch** OF **Duntourin, Ilford, Essex,** YOU ARE A WINNER IN OUR INCREDIBLE COMPETITION.

There are no catches! Well, there are, but not those sort of catches, just the other ones, as it were.

Yes, **Graham,** you have won the chance of a lifetime, a chance to SEE the world, MEET wonderful people, ENJOY the wide open spaces!

And all you have to do, **Mr Gooch,** is accept our offer of a FREE DRINK and an opportunity to meet our experienced representatives who will be holding an informal and friendly meeting at **The Board Room, MCC Headquarters, Lord's Cricket Ground, London** on **Sunday** or anytime really, **Graham,** it would be lovely to see you. We can send a car and everything. God, please come.

In exchange for which you can claim your FREE PRIZE of one of the following:

- **Sponsored Ford car like the one you probably already have but with more gadgets and some leather seats**
- **Captaincy of Essex for ever**
- **Beard trimmer**

At our meeting we will simply INVITE YOU to consider the benefits of touring abroad this winter with the England Cricket Team. YES, we know Atherton's doing his best but he's not in the same class really, and the rest of them only turn it on once in a blue moon.

What we'll do for you as well as the bits already mentioned:

- **We'll bring out all the food you like on a privately chartered jet**
- **We'll not go to Pakistan**
- **We'll ask Billy Bonds to come out to keep you company – and that girl from the pub you've had your eye on since you and the wife went your separate ways, these things happen and we all understand.**

DON'T DELAY, REPLY TODAY: A GREAT OPPORTUNITY AWAITS YOU **Mr Mike Gatting**. Sorry ... **Mr Graham Gooch**.

BOX
TIPS

Batsmen around the world grow to love their boxes. They depend upon them at the wicket and they trust them always. When the cricket season is over, it can be a traumatic experience for a batsman to have to separate himself abruptly from his box. So what can you do with your box during the winter months? Here are some useful tips:

1 A box can make a good soap dish to keep by your bath.

2 Buying realistic surroundings for your pet fish can be expensive. A box in the fish tank can make your fish feel at home – just add a few pebbles and bring hours of amusement to your pathetic fish.

3 Next time your moggy starts crying for milk and you can't be bothered to go to the kitchen to find a saucer, get your box out of your kit bag and fill it with milk. Your cat will never notice the difference and you will have saved yourself some valuable time.

4 Boxes make excellent ash trays.

5 Dress up like one of TV's Gladiators. Your strapped-on box can give you the thong which no shop will sell. A great way to impress your kids.

6 Boxes are often seen as unhygenic during the summer. But in the winter, strap a box on to your face and cycle into work and everyone will think you are a Friend of the Earth.

The spring-box in action

7 Put your butter in a box at breakfast time.

8 Get two boxes, hit them together and you can make the sound of horses' hooves. Take yourself down to the BBC and within seconds you will be invited to join the world of showbiz.

9 Use your box as a plant pot and grow lots of plants in it. Avoid cannabis as this can give you a weird sensation when you are batting next year.

10 Several boxes – attached to the vital positions – allow hours of safe skateboarding fun.

Dear Miss Wildgoose,
Please f____ help me, you s____ old f____
I can't help f____ swearing and blowing my c___ lid. On every tour I find it real f___ hard to keep my s___ m_____ temper, you know? Jeez, I'm fed up.
Yours, Merv from Oz. The one with the twitchy moustache.

Dear Merv,
Frustrations must be released. If not on the field, then in the bedroom. I seem to remember handing out all kinds of relief to your fellow Aussies on past tours. Sadly, I can't be everywhere at once. If only I had another pair of legs

I'd open in Sydney.
Boom boom.
Love, Hilda. The one with the twitchy beard.
....

Dear Hilda,
I miss you, my darling. It has been so long since I hiked across your love mountains or potholed your carnal cave. Have you been saving yourself for me?
I must admit to one or two little indiscretions on my travels, but one tires of endlessly fending off the advances of young women. In the end I relent and let them have their pleasure of me. Forgive me, my angel, I long for you.
Yours, Dicky

Dear Harold,
I, too, must admit that I also succumbed to two indiscretions: (I) the New Zealand team and (2) the

South African squad. And their physios. And the bloke that packs their kits.
....

Dear Hilda,
Why must we endure that common oik as chairman of selectors? He didn't even go to a decent school.
Yours, Disgusted of Eton

Dear Disgusted,
Everyone knows that success in cricket is reliant on success between the sheets. Public schoolboys are renowned for their inadequacy. They're too busy doing it to each other. Ray Illingworth, on the other hand, is the best shag I've ever had.
....

Wildgoose

he important issues and also does a lot of shagging

Dear Hilda,
Are you free on Friday, my sweet?
Love, Ray

Dear Ray,
You bring the key, I'll bring the turf.

· ·

Dear Miss Wildgoose,
Some of my friends are a little tired of what appear to be endless *doubles entendres* in which you compare cricket to the sexual act. What have you got to say for yourself?
Yours, Victor

Dear Victor,
Believe me, I never mix the two. It's for you to work out which is which. Incidentally, I always thought you were better at one than the other.

· ·

Dear Miss Wildgoose,
Why did Chris Lewis shave his head in the West Indies?
Yours, W Ashandgo

Dear W,
So that he could not only play like a little prick, but also look like one.

· ·

Dear Miss Wildgoose,
While we're discussing matters tonsorial, isn't it about time Ian Botham got rid of that stupid haircut, grew back his sideburns and lost the moustache?
Yours, Tim O'Tay

Dear Tim,
Definitely ... but who's going to tell him?

· ·

Dear Miss Wildgoose,
We all know you have had more cricketers than Mike Gatting has had hot dinners (steady on – Hilda), but have you ever been pleasured by a cricket writer?
Respect, D Pringle

Dear D,
'Pleasured' is not quite the word, though the sight of Martin Johnson naked save for his snakeskin winkle-picker boots was fairly amusing. And I am reminded of seeing several young things padding around St Lawrence Gap during the historic

Barbados
test wearing T-shirts bearing the legend 'Scyld Berry Popped My Cherry'.

· ·

Dear Miss Wildgoose,
Despite his recent performances for England, is Tony Adams a donkey or what?
Yours, Tel Boy, Mayfair

Dear Tel Boy,
Four legs, straw hat, carries children on his back on Blackpool beach. He's a donkey. But I think you should have written to 'Shoot!'.

· ·

Dear Miss W,
What did you make of all the fuss regarding Imran Khan and the revelations that he lifted the seam on several occasions?
Yours, W A

Dear W,
Imran can rub up my seam anytime he wants.

· ·

1 All-rounder, bowls, and bats a tiny bit, likes to field on or near the boundary. Quite good arm (three bounces to keeper or thereabouts). Enthusiasm makes up for lack of talent.

FACT **Very attractive wife, who is very active behind the scenes. She's a great favourite of the skip.**
....

2 Gladstone Small look alike, puts visual aggression in the side.

FACT **Local doctor who bowls the occasional slow over, bats where convenient, a thoroughly pleasant chap.**
....

3 Bowler. Gives the illusion of being pacy by sheer bulk.

THE ANATOMY OF
A CLUB TEAM

FACT Incredibly long run-up leading to a military medium climax. In fact, a complete trundler.

....

4 Vice-Captain, elder statesman, misses the turning wickets ... Likes to think he's skip's right-hand man.

FACT Club bore, on every committee, vets all new proposed members in case of threat to the club's status quo.

....

5 Bats at number 4. Domestic science teacher, so has time to run under 16 team which son is captain of ...

FACT Makes sure no 'riff-raff' element gets into the club. Also discourages any smarty (talent) from breaking through to threaten the first team regulars.

....

6 Seamer. Ladies hairdresser, always first in, last out of showers.

FACT Club's best bowler, zips the ball through like a whippet from hell. Deceiving erratic three-hop run-up.

....

7 Skipper's boy, so appearance is ignored. Lovely lad.

FACT Very spoiled, wouldn't stand a chance of selection or club membership except for the family ties. Most naturally gifted player in team.

....

8 Club utility player.

FACT Cuts pitch, paints pavilion, organizes whist drives, cleans skip's BMW. Club gossip, a complete toe-rag.

....

9 Skipper. Opening bat, opening bowler, first slip, umpire and after-dinner speaker at club dos.

FACT Very successful businessman (secondhand cars). Has rancho-style bungalow next to ground. Donated new shower unit in home team's dressing room. Claim to fame – once sat three tables away from Derek Pringle in a local bistro and shared the same urinal that evening.

....

10 Wicketkeeper. Guardian of the timbers for last 30 years.

FACT Local bank manager and club treasurer, say no more! Still walks with a slight limp due to a flying bail in 1963.

....

11 Bat 2-11. Someone once said there was a very slight resemblance to Ian Botham ... he's milked it ever since.

FACT Name is actually Dennis. Brother-in-law is a printer, very useful for skip and club.

....

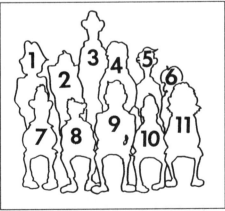

ANY RESEMBLANCE TO PERSONS LIVING OR DEAD IS PURELY ON PURPOSE.

AROUND THE Grounds

Every test match has a different atmosphere and every test match wicket has a different playing surface. In Adelaide, the lush wide blade grass makes for a true batting wicket.

At the Bourda in Georgetown, the incessant rain means that the pitch is largely baked mud, affording a rather dead low bounce.

But at Headingley, it's a different story. As a batsman you are as liable to get a shooter that scuttles along the ground as you are a spitting temple cruncher. It's very much a 'result' pitch and eight of the last ten tests played at Headingley have produced a 'result'. (The other two were badly affected by rain.)

It is a record of which Headingley groundsman, Keith Boyce, is very proud and a boon for advocates of 'positive cricket'. *The Googly* asked Keith the secret of his pitch preparation.

'For me the secret is to simulate the wear and tear of any municipal pitch in England. That way you get a wicket true to the real essence of English cricket,' says Boyce.

'Two weeks before a test match we stage a local fête on the ground. I like to put the bouncy castle on a good length so you get lots of kids' footprints nearby. Then I get my kids to cycle about the pitch in the evening before letting my four great danes roam the wicket a couple of days before the match. A bit of dogshit really adds to the unpredictability. We also like to adopt appropriate pitch maintenance techniques during the match. Not for us the light and heavy rollers but instead a choice between my brother-in-law's caravan being parked on it or a couple of kids let loose on spacehoppas.'

The TCCB has not always been happy with Keith's pitch preparation. No test since 1979 has lasted more than two and a half days and the TCCB estimate to have lost over £34,000,000 in potential gate receipts. But Boyce is unrepentant, 'So it makes the game a lottery. But at least it gives England an even chance!'

Over the years, the hill at Lord's has become more pronounced

106

BARTON-CUM-TORY
CRICKET AND SOCIAL CLUB

Rules for women's cricket

1. Try to leave your cars parked neatly at the far end of the club so that male members can park close to the clubhouse.

2. Women are allowed to use the cricket pitch on the second Wednesday of every month provided the male members do not need it for putting practice or bar-b-q-s.

3. When you are on the cricket ground, try not to use the flat bit in the middle where the men play.

4. You may want to pull the boundary ropes in a bit (tidily) as you cannot throw or hit the ball very far.

5. Remember to allow yourselves plenty of time for the tea interval. I am sure you will want to get a head start on making the sandwiches and tea and cakes for yourselves as you do so marvellously for the male members when we play.

6. If lady players intend to use the group bath after a game, would they please inform the social secretary prior to doing so.

7. Please note that the Ladies' locker room door must remain unlocked at all times for security reasons.

8. The social secretary politely asks all lady members to thoroughly clean and scrub all walls, floors, benches, corridors, toilets, club room carpets, windows and front drive after each game.

9. Personal hygiene: Is your silly mid-on or your wicketkeeper padding up? Then please ask them to avoid whites and to wear a sensible pair of dark, heavy tweed-type trousers. And perhaps even an overcoat.

10. As the social secretary is always keen to help lady members, the social secretary will gladly take any warm, slightly soiled bras belonging to lady members away for washing.

11. The bat is the long thin thing made of wood with a handle at one end.

Thank you for your attention.

G. H. Tewkesbury

G. H. Tewkesbury
Social Secretary
Barton-cum-Tory Cricket and Social Club

Aquarius (20 Jan - 18 Feb)

Tell me, Aquarius, why do you bother? You were born at a lousy time of the year, you can't bowl to save your life and those batting gloves with great naff blocks of foam over the knuckles went out with Tony Greig. This will be a terrible month for you if Saturn, Mars and Uranus have anything to do with it. Stay at home with a good book.

Pisces (19 Feb - 20 Mar)

Your fabled Piscean persistence is likely to pay off this month. On the 10th you'll win a small prize in a Test Match Special quiz, the 15th will bring good weather for that picnic on Hampstead Heath you've been planning since April and on the 21st it's a fair chance you'll be asked to open the batting for England in the final test against Pakistan.

Aries (21 Mar - 20 Apr)

Love is in the air for rams. Pack more than your usual supply of abdominal protectors when you go down to the game on Saturday, and remember: clear and unambiguous calling is the key to many a record-breaking partnership.

Taurus (21 Apr - 20 May)

It's drizzling, your flannels are half an inch too short and your wife has left you for a thrusting young medium-pacer.

Don't worry, Taureans, the planets will fall right for you in the end.

Gemini (c & b Capricorn – 8)

This is your last chance, Gemini. You were awful at mid-off last week, letting through three boundaries and dropping a sitter, and, quite frankly, it's likely to be some considerable time before I see a more lamentable display of batting. Call yourself a sign of the Zodiac? If you can't get it together this month I'll just have to drop you down the order and move Sagittarius up to number five. Got that?

Cancer (22 Jun - 22 Jul)

This is the big one. On Monday you'll inherit half of Sussex. Thursday will bring you news of a long-awaited promotion and to cap it all, you're about to fall in love as you've never fallen in love before. The bad news is that this is going to play merry hell with your bowling average.

Leo (23 Jul - 22 Aug)

Remember that dilemma you were agonizing over last month? Well the answer is: wait, wait ... yes, come on ... NO! GO BACK! ... OK, come on then. Two there. YOUR CALL. Your call! Sorry – look I said it was your call.

Virgo (23 Aug - 22 Sept)

You chatty, gregarious Virgoans are going

Stars

to have a great few weeks. Everybody seems to want to get to know you. Beautiful people just gravitate towards you at parties. Runs stream effortlessly from your bat and that boil (you know, that embarrassing one that's hampering your delivery stride) – well you're going to wake up on Tuesday and – ping! – it's going to have disappeared.

Scorpio (23 Oct - 21 Nov)

Bad news; getting up on Tuesday morning you'll discover a rather revolting little boil has erupted in an awkward spot. That's going to make it difficult to bowl on Saturday, I'm afraid. You'll be wondering why all the Virgoans you know are so bloody cheerful.

Sagittarius (22 Nov - 20 Dec)

You can't play cricket this month. There may be a good reason for that – you might be American, for example, or just plain unco-ordinated – but I reckon it's because Pluto's passing through Jupiter and frankly that always spooks Sagittarians.

Capricorn (21 Dec - 19 Jan)

If you've ever felt like going for it – you know, really letting it rip – this could be the month for it. Take the long run-up and screw the hamstring injury: you're only young once. Avoid Scorpions – tread on one of those and you might never bowl again.

WHY THE LORD'S TAVERNERS ARE CRAP

I

If I wanted to pay good money to see eleven clapped-out fools fanny around on a pitch, I'd go to a Test Match.

II

The most famous faces in the programme never turn up.

III

Two 'That's Life' presenters, four fat ex-cricketers and that gimp off 'Emmerdale' do not constitute a 'Celebrity XI' in anyone's book.

IV

Not only do they let Henry Kelly play, they let him bloody commentate as well.

V

We pay to get in, have to buy all our food, drink and raffle tickets then sit on the boundary while they knock back the Mumm and canapés. How hilarious.

VI

We don't ask people to turn up and watch us play badly, so why do we do it for them?

As a mark of our respect, THE GOOGLY has arranged a special Cricket Match to take place next summer:

LORD'S TAVERNERS CELEBRITY XI

vs

WEST INDIES.

We've had a quiet word with Curtley.

Zimbabwe

Zimbabwe's most momentous season to date may be over, but there is still plenty of work to be done by the administrators, who are currently engrossed in forming an internal first-class competition, the Mickey Mouse League, which will start next season.

The two teams to take part next season will be Matabeleland and Matabeleland B. Matches will last three days if all players can get the necessary time off work. Umpires will be provided by the batting team and teas are the responsibility of the wives of the home side.

There is also a one-day competition, the Matabeleland Cup. It will be a straight knock-out tournament of one game between the two Matabeleland teams. The winner takes the cup.

Bag carrying

Zimbabwe skipper, David Houghton highlighted the problems of making the step up to full ICC status: 'Persuading players to carry the team bag is very difficult now. They say that Mike Atherton and Richie Richardson don't have to, so why should they. We've had to implement stringent punishments, like collecting the match fees or filling in the score-book after the game.'

But Houghton is confident that the Zimbabweans can soon be a major force in Test cricket: 'We've got some tremendous players at the moment and some promising youngsters. When we've got a sightscreen, we'll be ready for anyone.'

'I *see* you've discovered that dodgy bit outside off-stump I warned you about'

· DAVID HOWARD·

COLLECT GOOGLY
Cricket Stars

Collect Googly cricket stars and stick them in your Googly cricket album. Each month The Googly will be printing a page that represents a page of your album. Just cut it out of the magazine each week and staple the pages together and hey presto you've got yourself an album absolutely free.

Then start collecting **GOOGLY CRICKET STARS** which are available in all newsagents in packs of six at the bargain price of just £2.50 per pack. If you get one player you've already got, then just swap it with a friend for one you haven't got. It's that simple.

Each pack contains six full-colour portraits of the world's cricket stars. A complete set in your album will make a wonderful collector's item.

So, to get the ball rolling, here is page one of your album – the full Sri Lanka squad.

Chewingumunderthesofa

Kayakrace

Bringandbuysale

Oxtungsarnie

Hihosilva

Chickeninabasket

Singersewingmachine

Scantillicladtillergirlie

Pandalingerie

Dogturdinashagpile

Candilwickbedspread

Wankmybudgie

English Umpires Are Randiest Men in the World IT'S OFFICIAL

English umpires can't wait to get their white coats off so they can jump into bed with young maidens — according to a new shock report.

One anonymous maiden told us: 'My husband, Henry, umpires every Sunday and wants sex every other night of the week and sometimes before breakfast.

'He always refers to his cricket when we are making love. He rips off my slip, loosens up and then lets fly with a couple of real quick ones. What's more, he always enforces the follow on.'

Sex expert, Rosemary Pimple, says there is a direct link between randiness and being an umpire. For some reason, very randy men are attracted to becoming umpires.

'Many fantasize when they are at square leg. Being an umpire is a hard job. Standing around for hours builds up sexual desires. Some umpires find it hard to forget work — even when they are having sex. Some insist on being videoed so they can watch the action replay and assess their own performance.'

The MCC is to set up a special umpire sex counselling service to try to help the men in white coats cool off and keep their minds firmly on cricket.

'How about a bit of ball-tampering?'

THE GOOGLY'S GUIDE TO
RIDICULOUS Middle Names

Devon **Eugene** Malcolm
Allan **Esmond** Warner
Ole **Henrik** Mortensen
Nicholas **Verity** Knight
Stephen **Royston** Barwick
Robert Damien **Bale** Croft
Cardigan **Adolphus** Connor
Matthew **Valentine** Fleming
Neil **Royston** Taylor
Nigel **Edwin** Briers
Peter **Nash** Hepworth
Jason **Calvin** Pooley
Philip **Clive Roderick** Tufnell
Curtly **Elconn Lynwall** Ambrose
Nicholas **Grant Billson** Cook
Gregory **Wentworth** Mike
Franklyn **Dacosta** Stephenson
Adrianus **Pelrus** Van Troost
Antony Charles **Shackleton** Pigott
Duncan John **Richardson** Martindale
Piran Christopher **Laity** Holloway
Adrian Roger **Kirshaw** Pierson
Gladstone **Cleophas** Small
Neil Michael **Knight** Smith

AlecStewart's GUIDE TO THE French Revolution

'The whole bloody mess was to do wiv dosh. Louis XVI's treasury didn't 'ave none. So in 1789, the Fird Estate, who was selected by the people, put togevver a new constitution. There was no boss, no guvnor and no gaffer. Total farce. In Paris a mob of 'ooligans stormed the Bastille. In 1792 a declaration of the Republic, and next year Louis XVI was sawn off.'

THE IAN SALISBURY Legspin
M·A·S·T·E·R·C·L·A·S·S

In an earlier issue, Ian described that subtlest of variations, the Flipper. Today he gives his expert tips on the Full Toss.

The Full Toss can be a tremendous weapon if used sparingly – say two or three times an over. But don't be tempted to overdo it. I tried four an over recently and the batsmen were beginning to read it!

The secret of success is concealment, so always try to make it look as if you had no control whatsoever over the delivery. You can build this illusion by cursing, rubbing dirt on your hands, or using my own speciality – alternating it with rank long hops ... **(At this point Ian was dragged away screaming by men in white coats and put on a flight to the West Indies.)**

DAVID HOLLAND

Thussock sends down a 'flipper'

Flannel-Arsed Wasters

They make my cuffing blood boil, they really do. No, not those grease-balls out on the pitch, I'm talking about rich people.

In particular, those ugly, lemon-faced gits that clog up the ground with their Burberry blazers, MCC umbrellas and hospitality boxes.

You know the ones; they waltz around the ground wearing those brown shoes with the dots in as if someone's blasted them with shot-gun pellets. Their main topic of conversation is about what sort of chlorine they're going to put in their cuffing swimming pool this summer.

They blow their noses on a tenner, get their chauffeur to bring them a scorecard, then mince off into the nearest box or tent for some free bloody champagne.

They're the sort of people you see in Jermyn Street when you're being sick after a night out at the Cockney Tavern.

While decent folk queue up for forty-five minutes to buy a kebab that looks like something that's been dragged out of a car accident, these privileged pansies are on a velvet couch having caviar ladled into their ever-open gobs by rent boys on loan from Westminster.

So, if you're more likely to see the inside of a thermos than the inside of a hospitality tent, let me cheer you up a bit.

There ain't a sweet trolley, punch bowl or gravy boat in one of those places that hasn't been subject to some form of unpleasant yet very imaginative act of 'Rindery'.

Not so much hair in the soup as Fisons in the Foie Gras.

After a hard day of turf-fondling, me and the juniors always clear up the fertilizers, worm casts, tins of marker paint and so on, then creep round the back of the tents to do a bit of novel cuisine of our own.

Let me tell yer, there's nothing like a bit of Benlate in the bouillabaise to wipe the smile off some bloke who's never seen the inside of a comprehensive or a borstal (much the same thing these days).

Finally, as I add a dash of dung to the Pimms, this is Chef Harry Rind reminding cricketers everywhere ...

'Get off my cuffing pitch, you flannel-arsed wasters!'

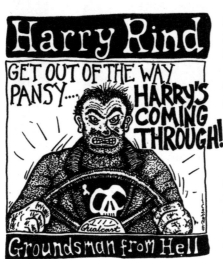

Harry Rind

GET OUT OF THE WAY PANSY.... HARRY'S COMING THROUGH!

Groundsman from Hell

Trouble at MILL

The Googly eavesdrops on Lancashire skipper Mike Watkinson's team talk.

Mike Watkinson: Right, lads, we've had a few problems this season, but we've got a lot of captains in this team so it makes sense to use all your brains.

Warren Hegg: Well, I think -

Watkinson: Not you, Hegg. You've never captained anyone, you daft toilet roll. Where do you think we've been going wrong this season, Neil?

Neil Fairbrother: Well, the problem last year was that there was no team spirit.

Jason Gallian: Bollocks.

Fairbrother: What would you know about it, Gallian? You're not even Lancastrian.

Jason Gallian: Yeah, I'm Australian. We know about winning. We're tough. That's how I got results at Oxford last year.

John Crawley: Not against Cambridge you didn't.

Gallian: Shut up, Crawley. Just cos you went to Atherton's school.

Watkinson: All right, calm down, lads. Wasim, you've captained Pakistan. What did you do when things weren't going well?

Wasim Akram: Sack Javed.

Watkinson: Right. Anything else?

Wasim: Got a bottle top? I'll show you.

Graham Lloyd: My dad was captain of Lancashire.

Watkinson: Doesn't count, Lloydy. It's up to you, Athers. You managed to get England winning again. What should we do?

Mike Atherton: See if you can change the fixture list. Give Lord's a ring.

Watkinson: Right.

Atherton: Ask for 17 matches against New Zealand.

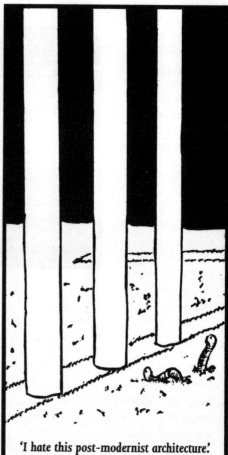

'I hate this post-modernist architecture.'

The MCC PLUM

The MCC has produced a limited range of <u>SPECIAL PLUMS</u> as part of its campaign to improve communications with cricket fans everywhere.

Cricket followers are encouraged to buy the plums (£1.50 + pp); place them in their mouths and start a conversation with a member of the MCC. The <u>MCC PLUM</u> is guaranteed to break down barriers between members of the MCC and everyone else who watches cricket.

Sid Spanner says:

'I've been going t'Lord's for years and I've never been able to talk to those MCC toffs. So I thought I would give this <u>MCC PLUM</u> a try - and it worked wonders. As soon as I had stuffed the <u>MCC PLUM</u> in my gob, I could talk to anyone wearing one of those silly ties. It were like arriving in a new country.'

The Secretary of the MCC says:

'The <u>MCC PLUM</u> was the first step forward in a major communications programme to make the public more accessible to members of the MCC.'

A Handful of Dust...

AMAZING
ICC Annual Meeting

Those historic ICC decisions in full:

- Sir Brian Dribble re-elected as Chairman for 20-year period
- Australia's Colin Lawley to replace New Zealand's Paul Johnson on ICC umpires' panel
- 90 over a day minimum for Tests to remain (proposal to increase to 91 was defeated)
- Application for matches involving Pakistan 'A' in 2003-4 World Cup to be given official one-day international status deferred until next year
- Isle of Wight elected associate members of ICC. Applications from Italy and America deferred
- Mohammed Ahmed to join ICC Committee with immediate effect
- As for sledging, slow over rates and ball-tampering – deferred

DAVID HOLLAND.

Nepal exploit home advantage in the ICC Trophy

MY KIND OF DAY

by Philip de Freitas

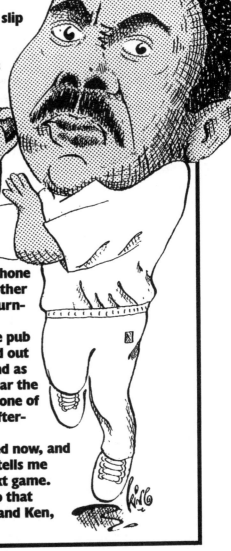

I'm up and straight into the shower most mornings, making sure I don't slip on the soap and pull my hamstring like I did on the last tour in India.

On match days, I spend a few minutes trying to remember who I'm playing for. It used to be Leicestershire and Lancashire but now it's Derbyshire (I think).

If I don't have a game, I like to go down to my local at lunchtime and play with the darts team. Our skipper can never decide whether he wants me in the team or not, so often I'll turn up and he'll say I've been dropped.

So I'll go home again and the second I'm through the front door the phone will go and Skip'll be saying one of the other lads has dropped out, so would I mind turning up after all?

I always say OK and I'll go back to the pub but usually whoever it was who dropped out has turned up, so I go off home again and as I'm putting my keys in the door I can hear the phone ringing and it's Skip again saying one of the lads has to go back to work in the afternoon so would I mind coming back?

So I say OK and arrive, a bit knackered now, and not able to throw properly, so the Skip tells me afterwards that I'm dropped for the next game. But if Les can't play cos he's got to go to that sales conference, then it's between me and Ken, so that cheers me up.

Full Pitch

by RICK HORNBY

The Googly reproduces here exclusive extracts of the best-selling rites of passage story of a young cricket fan.

Dennis Breakwell pushed through a flat top spinner and Graham Roope ran a leg bye to backward square leg. It was the first ball of professional cricket I'd ever watched and I was hooked. My love affair with cricket and more particularly with Surrey had begun.

I was 12 years old and smitten and watching John Edrich bash Somerset's bowlers about was nearly as much fun as me 'bashing the bishop'. My face was at that tender age bound together by pustulating acne and was the focus of considerable classroom mirth but at The Oval I found a new bunch of similarly zit-ridden youths and it was in the bosom of these sad losers that my passage into manhood took place. My father left my mother for the Swedish au pair who lived next door and my sister was in the full throes of her bulimia but I was happy - Surrey were through to the next stage of the Benson & Hedges Cup!

August 18th 1974
Yorkshire v Surrey

My first trip away from home. We took the coach bound for a drizzling Leeds. I had two flasks of oxtail soup, some peanut butter sandwiches my mother had made me, my scorebook, and my trusty multicolour jumbo biro. What an adventure! My friend John produced a well-thumbed copy of *Health and Efficiency* just outside Luton. Soon the sweet smell of dried semen on nylon pac-a-mac filled the air.

Girls had long remained a mystery to me until that trip to Headingley. But there I met Avril Sidebottom, Social Secretary of Yorkshire C C Junior Supporters. We got on famously chatting about cricket records and things. I showed her my photo album of snaps taken from various parts of The Oval. I have to say that after two days sitting next to her I had become transfixed by the two pert breasts under her kagool - they reminded me of the gas-ometers at The Oval and at teatime on the third day she whispered in my ear. 'Hey, Rick, how about us lying down there by the tarpaulins and seeing what sweating under the covers really means.' I said: 'And miss Lonsdale Skinner reach his maiden first class fifty, you must be joking!' Women! And I thought she was a cricket fan.

July 23rd 1980

Hampshire v Surrey

University imposed a trial separation on my love affair with Surrey. Away from my spiritual home under the gasometers in SE17 I escaped into a monk-like search for the interior spirit. I spent hours alone in my room contemplating an existence away from my beloved Surrey. I took some comfort in that at nights when the light hit it from certain angles, my penis looked like Geoff Arnold's head. But it was scarcely sufficient for a man with a 62-day-a-year Oval habit.

It was a difficult time for me - my father had killed my mother with a Kenwood food mixer and I'd lost a leg in a freak pedalo accident in Corfu, but we'd had a decent season in the John Player League and the second XI was showing potential.

August 9th 1992

Surrey v Lancashire

The day had started badly. I received a phone call to say my sister and grandmother had been killed in a motorway pile-up. She was driving Granny to the hospital to have a colostomy bag fitted. And five minutes later my girlfriend of six years standing announced she was carrying the secret lovechild of the bloke next door - a chap called Bevan, an unemployed carpet salesman from Pontypool. And blow me when I get to the ground Surrey are 32 for 5 with Keith Medlycott on a pair! When it rains, it pours. Lucky we've got such good covers at The Oval!

Rick Hornby is now writing about what he did on his summer holidays for a Sunday newspaper.

'When I bowls a Chinaman, I bowls a bloody Chinaman!'

° DAVID HOLLAND °

123

Talking

I'm constantly told that our young-sters don't play cricket in our schools any more so I ventured through the gates of my local school to find out for myself. Three chalked stumps against the wall of the boys' latrine suggested cricket was far from dead but on further enquiry I found that the playing fields had been sold off and become a Bejam hypermarket and that the master in charge of sports was in fact a mistress who wore a stud in her nose and her les-bianism on her sleeve.

When I was at school - in the days when 'good smack' meant a healthy slap round the thighs rather than something to snort - the schoolyard was full of boys who were as keen as mustard to get into the nets. 'Come on, Biffo, bugger lat. prep! Come and show me your chinaman,' we would shout. But not now. Walking down a corridor of my local school, a waif of a girl said, 'Hello, Grandad, I'll give you a gobble for a fiver.' No idea what she was talking about - it's a whole different language these days. Bloody Shirley Williams - I blame her. Comprehensive schools have wrecked society and cricket too. It just goes to show you should never put a woman in charge of anything - except maybe a tea urn in a village pavilion. It's all such a shame ...

I'm sick and tired of hearing the plaintive cry from the spineless workshy ponces that call themselves cricketers in the 1990s of 'We play too much cricket.' Who are they kidding? Seventeen four-day matches and a few pyjama romps - call that a cricket season? Tich Freeman would have bowled 9,000 overs by the end of May. Dear, dear Tich ... only 4ft 8ins but a devil in white, spinning a web with those long strong fingers till arthritis caught up with him. If only a hospital could have got to those fingers in time - bloody NHS, absolute shambles, I blame Clem Attlee and that Welsh git Nye Bevan. It's such a shame ...

Logos on the outfield, logos on flannels, logos on sightscreens ... What next? Fielders in sandwich boards? There was a time when cricketers played for pleasure and spectators paid to watch their skills not to skive off work on some corporate hospitality beano. That was a time when players wore proper caps not these bloody baseball things, when players walked rather than sledged, when the umpire's decision was final not an invitation to argue, when real ale tasted of hops and not carbonated goat's piss. Now it's all gone. It's all gone. We're left with nothing. Oh how I miss Gubby's bowling or Fender's batting, and Tizer, and Joyce Grenfell, and men wearing hats, and Woolies pick 'n' mix counters, and policemen on bikes, and raindrops on roses, and whiskers on kittens, and bright copper kettles, and warm woollen mittens, and brown paper packages tied up with string ...

BY

E W Swansong

Cricket

NEW Cricketing Swearwords

● Avoid accusations of sledging ● Insult senior officials without them knowing

● No more embarrassing slow-motion replays of your obscenities

Dexter (noun): General term of abuse. As in ' He's a complete dexter.'

Gatt (verb): Can be used as a reference to over-indulgence. As in 'I really gatted out at that curry house.'

Twose (noun): Gentlemen's unmentionables. As in 'That one lifted and caught him right in the twose.'

Younis (noun): Rhyming slang, for example: 'I just saw Devon in the shower. What a waqar!'

Fletcher (noun): See Dexter.

Bearded Wonder (noun): Ladies' unmentionables.

Bird (noun): Rhyming slang, for example: 'If you ask me, the MCC are a right bunch of harolds.'

Hobbs (noun): (plural): See Twose.

Geoff (noun): Unpleasant, self-centred person, for example: 'He's a right bearded wonder that gatting geoff.'

Wessels (noun): (pl): Pubic hair. As in 'His box nestles in the wessels.'

Roebuck (noun): Rhyming slang, for example: 'Ah! How I like a nice communal bath after a long, hard, sweaty day in the field ... I, ahm, haven't told you this but ... you're a good looking bloke, you know ... listen, no one's about ... do you, er, fancy a peter?'

COMPETITION

THROUGH THE KEYHOLE

From the following pictorial clues, can you piece together the identity of this well-known cricketer?

1 This is the house of an England test batsman

4 And ten boxes of these in the corner of his living room

5 He keeps a lot of this under the mattress in the spare room

2 And this is his driveway

Who is it?

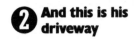

3 We found this in his cricket bag in the hallway

6 And for £500 in hard ECUs or Krugerrands, he'll let you shag his missus

Send your answers to:
....
Robin Smith Competition, The Googly,
29b Meteor Street, London SW11 5NZ

Subscribe today!

If you have enjoyed reading **The Googly Annual,** why not subscribe to the magazine? Only **£6** for six issues

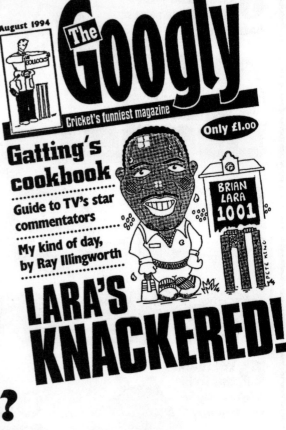

August 1994

The Googly

Cricket's funniest magazine

Only £1.00

Gatting's cookbook

Guide to TV's star commentators

My kind of day, by Ray Illingworth

BRIAN LARA 1001

LARA'S KNACKERED!